W9-AQG-559

Microsoft®
Windows® 2000
Active Directory™ Services

Lab Manual

PUBLISHED BY
Microsoft Press
A Division of Microsoft Corporation
One Microsoft Way
Redmond, Washington 98052-6399

Library of Congress Cataloging-in-Publication Data
MCSE Training Kit--Microsoft Windows 2000 Active Directory Services / Microsoft Corporation.
        p. cm.
    Includes index.
    ISBN 0-7356-0999-3
    ISBN 0-7356-1045-2 (Academic Learning Series)
    ISBN 0-07-285068-X (McGraw-Hill Ryerson)
    1. Electronic data processing personnel--Certification. 2. Microsoft
software--Examinations--Study guides.   3. Directory services (Computer network
technology)--Examinations--Study guides.   I. Microsoft Coporation.

    QA76.3 .M33452   2000
    005.4'469--dc21   99-059498

Printed and bound in the United States of America.

3 4 5 6 7 8 9   QWT   7 6 5 4 3

Distributed by McGraw-Hill Ryerson.

A CIP catalogue record for this book is available from the British Library.

Microsoft Press books are available through booksellers and distributors worldwide. For further information about international editions, contact your local Microsoft Corporation office or contact Microsoft Press International directly at fax (425) 936-7329. Visit our Web site at www.microsoft.com/mspress. Send comments to *tkinput@microsoft.com*.

Acquisitions Editor: Thomas Pohlman
Argosy Publishing Project Manager: Daniel Rausch
Series Editor: Julie Miller
Technical Editors: Kurt Musselman and Steve Perry

Author: Douglas H. Steen

SubAssy Part No. X09-13148
Body Part No. X08-46909

Introduction

This Lab Manual supplements the *ALS: Microsoft Windows 2000 Active Directory Services* textbook. The labs in this manual are designed to be performed in a classroom environment by a group of students under the supervision of an instructor. This is in contrast to the hands-on exercises in the textbook, which are designed to be performed outside the classroom. The labs in this manual and in the hands-on exercises in the textbook are an essential part of students' training. The opportunity to explore the menus, options, and responses will ensure an understanding of the appropriate use of Active Directory.

The labs in this manual do not precisely mirror the exercises in the textbook. Domain names, user names, IP addresses, shared resources, and other specific references in this manual are different than those in the textbook. Also, because each institution's local networking requirements are unique, there might be slight differences between the names and addresses in your classroom and those appearing in these labs. Your Instructor will explain any differences.

The labs are performed in a classroom that is set up as an isolated network. The instructor computer (named NewYork) is a Microsoft Windows 2000 domain controller. The instructor computer includes shared folders that contain programs and data files that support the labs.

The Microsoft Certified Professional (MCP) exams are demanding in both the knowledge and the hands-on experience they require. Students preparing for the Microsoft certification tests can increase their competence by gaining first-hand experience in the implementation and management of Active Directory. One of the best ways to become confident in the use of Active Directory Services is to complete all the assigned labs in this manual as well as the hands-on exercises in the textbook.

Lab Navigation

The labs in this manual and the exercises in the textbook use drop-down menus to demonstrate how to navigate through Windows interface elements, such as Microsoft Management Console (MMC). There are rare instances when drop-down menus are not available, and in these cases, explicit instructions are provided for using context menus. You can activate an object's context menu by right-clicking the object.

The labs and textbook exercises use the Windows default double-click setting: double-click to open an item (single-click to select). Do not configure the computers to use the optional single-click to open an item (point to select) setting.

Lab 1: Joining a Microsoft Windows 2000 Domain

Objectives

After completing this lab, you will be able to

- Configure a computer running Microsoft Windows 2000 Server to join a Windows 2000 domain.
- View the changes to a computer running Windows 2000 Server after joining a Windows 2000 domain.

Before You Begin

Before working on this lab, you must have

- Knowledge about the difference between a workgroup and a domain.
- Experience logging on and off Windows 2000.

Estimated time to complete this lab: 15 minutes

Exercise 1
Joining a Windows 2000 Domain

In this exercise, you will configure your stand-alone computer running Windows 2000 Server to join the instructor's domain (contoso.msft).

▶ **To view the configuration prior to joining the Windows 2000 domain**

1. Log on to your computer (running) as Administrator with a password of **password**.

2. Click Start, point to Programs, point to Administrative Tools, and then click Computer Management.

   The Computer Management console starts.

3. In the console tree, expand the Local Users And Groups node, and then select the Groups node.

4. In the Details pane, double-click Administrators.

5. In the Administrators Properties dialog box, note the members of the Administrators group.

6. Click the Cancel button.

7. Close the Computer Management console.

▶ **To add your computer to the instructor's domain (contoso.msft)**

1. Right-click the My Computer icon, and then click Properties.

2. In the System Properties dialog box, on the Network Identification tab, click the Properties button.

3. Under Member Of, select the Domain option button, type **contoso.msft**, and then click OK.

4. In the Domain Username And Password dialog box, in the Name text box, type **Administrator**.

5. In the Password text box, type **password**, and then click OK.

   A Network Identification message box welcomes you to the contoso.msft domain.

6. Click OK.

   A Network Identification message box informs you that you must reboot your computer for the changes to take effect.

7. Click OK.

8. Click OK to close the System Properties dialog box.

9. In the System Settings Change dialog box, click the Yes button to restart the computer.

   The computer restarts.

▶ **To log on to the Windows 2000 domain**

1. Log on to the contoso domain as Administrator with a password of **password**.

2. In the Windows 2000 Configure Your Server dialog box, clear the Show This Screen At Startup check box, and then close the dialog box.

▶ **To view the configuration after joining the Windows 2000 domain**

1. Click Start, point to Programs, point to Administrative Tools, and then click Computer Management.

   The Computer Management console starts.

2. In the console tree, expand the Local Users And Groups node, and then select the Groups node.

3. In the Details pane, double-click Administrators.

   In the Administrators Properties dialog box, note the members of the Administrators group. How has the membership of the Administrators group changed since you joined the domain?

   _____

   _____

4. Click the Cancel button.

5. In the Details pane, double-click Users.

   In the Users Properties dialog box, note the members of the Users group. How has the membership of the Users group changed since you joined the domain?

   _____

   _____

6. Click the Cancel button.

7. Close the Computer Management console.

Lab 2: Applying Active Directory Concepts

Objectives

After completing this lab, you will be able to

- Determine an appropriate number of domains, trees, organizational units, sites, and domain controllers for a proposed Active Directory installation.
- Determine an appropriate structure for a Domain Name System (DNS) name-space, and an appropriate number of DNS name servers.
- Determine an appropriate number of global catalog servers.
- Devise a scheme for replication within sites and replication between sites.

Estimated time to complete this lab: 30 minutes

Exercise 1
Determining Active Directory
and DNS Namespace Structures

In this exercise, you will analyze the requirements of an organization so that you can recommend an Active Directory domain structure and a DNS namespace structure.

Scenario

Northwind Traders is an organization that is preparing to install Active Directory. The organization is headquartered in Kansas City and has branch offices located throughout North America. All the connections between locations have T1 or greater performance.

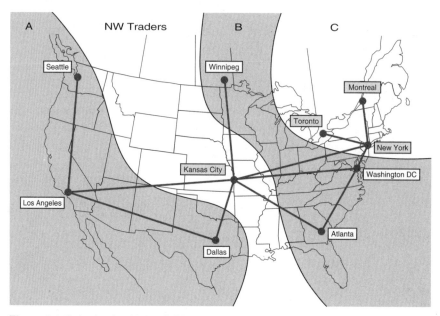

Figure 2.1 Organization Network Diagram

The offices in Los Angeles, Atlanta, and New York have local administrators who are responsible for the user accounts and resources in each of the respective locations. The other locations are administered from Los Angeles, Atlanta, or New York. The administrators in Kansas City can manage all locations.

The following table lists each location, the number of users at each location, and how each location is administered.

Location	Number Of Users	Region	Administered By
Kansas City	350	NWTraders	Self
Los Angeles	300	Region-A	Self, Kansas City
Atlanta	275	Region-B	Self, Kansas City
New York	280	Region-C	Self, Kansas City
Seattle	150	Region-A	Los Angeles
Dallas	175	Region-A	Los Angeles
Winnipeg	160	Region-B	Atlanta
Washington, D.C.	190	Region-B	Atlanta
Toronto	125	Region-C	New York
Montreal	110	Region-C	New York

▶ **To develop an Active Directory domain tree**

In the space provided below, draw an Active Directory domain tree that reflects the structure of the company.

▶ **To determine an appropriate number of Active Directory sites**

Your job is to recommend an Active Directory site structure for Northwind Traders, which wants to reduce the amount of network traffic associated with Active Directory. You can utilize 64 Kbps of network capacity between locations for Active Directory traffic.

1. Based on the information in the scenario, how many sites should you create and upon what do you base that number?

_____

_____

_____

2. What is the minimum number of domain controllers that you should install and upon what do you base that number?

_____

_____

_____

3. What is the minimum number of global catalog servers that you should install and upon what do you base that number?

_____

_____

► **To determine an appropriate DNS namespace and an appropriate number of DNS name servers**

Before you install Active Directory, you should devise a DNS namespace and determine an appropriate number of DNS name servers.

In the space provided below, draw a DNS domain namespace that reflects the structure of the company.

1. What is the relationship between the Active Directory domain structure and the DNS namespace?

_____

_____

2. What is the minimum number of DNS name servers that you should install and upon what do you base that number?

_____

_____

► **To create organizational units for Northwind Traders**

Northwind Traders has separate business divisions that are independent business units. Each location has a retail sales, a wholesale sales, and a distribution division. Each division must be able to administer its own resources.

In the space provided below, draw a set of organizational units (reflecting the company structure) within each domain.

Lab 3: Using the Active Directory Tools

Objectives

After completing this lab, you will be able to

- Install the Active Directory administrative tools on a stand-alone computer running Microsoft Windows 2000 Server.
- Use the Active Directory administrative tools to examine the instructor's domain (contoso.msft).
- Use Microsoft Management Console (MMC) to create custom consoles for performing Active Directory administrative tasks.
- Automate administrative tasks by using Task Scheduler.

Estimated time to complete this lab: 30 minutes

Exercise 1
Installing the Active Directory Administrative Tools

In this exercise, you will install the Active Directory administrative tools on your stand-alone computer running Windows 2000 Server.

▶   **To install the Active Directory administrative tools**

1. Log on to the contoso domain as Administrator with a password of **password**.

2. Click Start, and then click Run.

3. In the Open box, type **\\newyork\i386\adminpak.msi**, and then click OK.

    First the Windows installer starts, then the Windows 2000 Administration Tools Setup Wizard starts.

4. On the Welcome To The Windows 2000 Administration Tools Setup Wizard page, click Next.

5. Click the Finish button.

Exercise 2
Using the Active Directory Administrative Tools

In this exercise, you will use the standard Active Directory administrative consoles to examine the instructor's domain (contoso.msft).

▶ **To examine the users and groups currently in the domain**

1. Click Start, point to Programs, point to Administrative Tools, and then click Active Directory Users And Computers.

2. In the console tree, expand the Contoso.msft node, and then select the Users node.

3. In the Details pane, double-click Domain Admins.

4. In the Domain Admins Properties dialog box, open the Members tab.

   Note that Administrator is the only member of the Domain Admins group.

5. Open the Member Of tab.

   Note that Domain Admins is a member of the Administrators built-in group.

6. Click the Cancel button.

7. In the console tree, select the Built In node.

   Note the list in the Details pane. What is the difference between the groups listed in the Builtin folder and the groups listed in the Users folder?

   _____

   _____

   _____

▶ **To examine the computers currently in the domain**

1. In the console tree, select the Computers node.

2. In the Details pane, double-click *Computer* (where *Computer* is your assigned computer name).

3. In the *Computer* Properties dialog box, open the Operating System tab.

   Note the version and build number of Windows 2000 installed on your computer.

4. Open the Member Of tab.

   Note that your computer is a member of the Domain Computers group by default.

5. Click the Cancel button.

6. In the console tree, select the Domain Controllers node.

7. In the Details pane, double-click NEWYORK.

8. In the NEWYORK Properties dialog box, open the Member Of tab.

   Note that NEWYORK is a member of the Domain Controllers group by default.

9. Click the Cancel button.

10. Close the Active Directory Users And Computers console.

▶ **To examine the Active Directory sites and services**

1. Click Start, point to Programs, point to Administrative Tools, and then click Active Directory Sites And Services.

2. In the console tree, expand the Sites node.

3. Expand the Default-First-Site-Name node.

4. Select the Servers node.

   Explain why your server does, or does not, appear in the list of servers in the Details pane.

   _____

   _____

5. In the console tree, select the Inter-Site Transports node.

   What inter-site transport protocols are available in the Details pane?

   _____

   _____

6. Close the Active Directory Sites And Services console.

▶ **To examine the Active Directory domains and trusts**

1. Click Start, point to Programs, point to Administrative Tools, and then click Active Directory Domains And Trusts.

2. In the console tree, right-click the Contoso.msft node, and then click Properties.

3. In the Contoso.msft Properties dialog box, open the Trusts tab.

   What trust relationships currently exist and why?

   _____

   _____

   Between which entities would you create trust relationships by using this console?

   _____

   _____

4. Click the Cancel button.

5. In the console tree, right-click the Contoso.msft node, and then click Manage. The Active Directory Users And Computers console appears.

    What is another way of accomplishing this task?

    _____

    _____

6. Close the Active Directory Users And Computers console.
7. Close the Active Directory Domains And Trusts console.

Exercise 3
Creating a Custom MMC Console

In this exercise, you will create a custom MMC console on your stand-alone computer running Windows 2000 Server, and use the Active Directory administrative snap-ins to examine the instructor's domain (contoso.msft).

▶ **To create and save a custom console**

1. Click Start, and then click Run.

2. In the Open box, type **mmc**, and then click OK.

   MMC starts and displays an empty console.

3. On the Console menu, click Add/Remove Snap-In.

4. In the Add/Remove Snap-In dialog box, on the Standalone tab, click the Add button.

5. In the Add Standalone Snap-In dialog box, in the Snap-In column, select Active Directory Domains And Trusts, and then click the Add button.

6. In the Snap-In column, select Active Directory Schema, and then click the Add button.

7. In the Snap-In column, select Active Directory Sites And Services, and then click the Add button.

8. In the Snap-In column, select Active Directory Users And Computers, click the Add button, and then click the Close button.

9. In the Add/Remove Snap-In dialog box, click OK.

10. On the Console menu, click Options.

11. In the Options dialog box, in the Console Mode drop-down list, select User Mode—Limited Access, Single Window.

12. Select the Do Not Save Changes To This Console check box, and then click OK.

13. On the Console menu, click Save As, and save the console as **Active Directory Administration** on the desktop.

14. On the Console menu, click Exit.

▶ **To examine the instructor's domain (contoso.msft)**

1. On the desktop, double-click the Active Directory Administration icon.

2. In the console tree, expand the Active Directory Users And Computers node, expand the Contoso.msft node, and then select the Users node.

   Note the list of users and groups in the Details pane.

3. In the console tree, expand the Active Directory Sites And Services node, expand the Sites node, expand the Default-First-Site-Name node, and then select the Servers node.

Note the list of servers in the Details pane.

4. In the console tree, expand the Active Directory Domains And Trusts node, right-click the Contoso.msft node, and then click Properties.

Note the properties of the domain.

5. Click the Cancel button.

What is the difference between the console you created and the Active Directory consoles provided by Windows 2000?

_____

_____

▶ **To examine the schema of the instructor's domain (contoso.msft)**

1. In the console tree, expand the Active Directory Schema node, expand the Classes node, right-click the User node, and then click Properties.

2. In the User Properties dialog box, open the General tab.

Note the attributes that are described.

3. Open the Attributes tab.

What mandatory system attributes are listed for the user object (Tip: look in the Mandatory list box)?

_____

4. Click the Cancel button.

5. In the Details pane, click the Type column heading to sort the user object attributes by type.

Are any of the attributes listed in the Details pane mandatory attributes? If so, why weren't these attributes listed for the user object (Tip: look in the Source Class column)?

_____

_____

_____

_____

6. Why would you use the Active Directory Schema snap-in?

_____

_____

7. Close the Active Directory Administration console.

Exercise 4
Automating Administrative Tasks

In this exercise, you will create a scheduled task to back up your server.

▶ **To create a scheduled task**

1. Click Start, point to Programs, point to Accessories, point to System Tools, and then click Scheduled Tasks.

2. In the Scheduled Tasks window, double-click Add Scheduled Task.

   The Scheduled Task Wizard starts.

3. Click Next.

4. In the Application column, select Backup, and then click Next.

5. Select the Daily option button, and then click Next.

6. Accept the default time and day to start the task, and then click Next.

7. In the Enter The User Name text box, type **CONTOSO\Administrator**.

8. In the Enter The Password and Confirm Password text boxes, type **password**.

9. Click Next.

10. Select the Open Advanced Properties For This Task When I Click Finish check box, and then click the Finish button.

11. In the Backup dialog box, open the Settings tab.

    Notice the power management options at the bottom of the page.

12. Click the Cancel button.

▶ **To delete a scheduled task**

1. Click Start, point to Programs, point to Accessories, point to System Tools, and then click Scheduled Tasks.

2. In the Scheduled Tasks window, right-click Backup, and then click Delete.

3. In the Confirm File Delete dialog box, click the Yes button.

4. Close the Scheduled Tasks window.

Lab 4: Implementing Active Directory

Objectives

After completing this lab, you will be able to

- Install and configure DNS to support Active Directory.
- Convert a member server to a domain controller by installing Active Directory.
- Verify the installation of Active Directory.
- Create organizational units in Active Directory.

Before You Begin

To complete this lab, you will need the information in the following table. Ask your instructor to supply you with the information.

When you are asked for	Use
Classroom number	
IP address	
Domain name	

Estimated time to complete this lab: 60 minutes

Exercise 1
Installing DNS to Support Active Directory

In this exercise, you will analyze the requirements of Contoso, Ltd., and install DNS to support its Active Directory deployment.

Scenario

Contoso, Ltd., is preparing to install Microsoft Windows 2000 and Active Directory. You must install the first domain controller at your location within Contoso, Ltd. Before you can install the first domain controller, you must configure DNS to support Active Directory.

Each location within Contoso, Ltd., must be able to administer the accounts and resources for that location. In addition, the administrators in the headquarters office in New York must be able to administer all locations.

The following table shows the DNS namespace structure that has been developed for Contoso, Ltd. Your instructor will provide you with the value for x, which is your assigned classroom number.

Computer Name	Forward Lookup Zone	Network ID
Chicago	chicago-dom.contoso.msft	192.168.x
Atlanta	atlanta-dom.contoso.msft	192.168.x
Boston	boston-dom.contoso.msft	192.168.x
SanJose	sanjose-dom.contoso.msft	192.168.x
Montreal	montreal-dom.contoso.msft	192.168.x
Toronto	toronto-dom.contoso.msft	192.168.x
Vancouver	vancouver-dom.contoso.msft	192.168.x
Edmonton	edmonton-dom.contoso.msft	192.168.x
Paris	paris-dom.contoso.msft	192.168.x
Brussels	brussels-dom.contoso.msft	192.168.x
Madrid	madrid-dom.contoso.msft	192.168.x
London	london-dom.contoso.msft	192.168.x
Bonn	bonn-dom.contoso.msft	192.168.x
Rome	rome-dom.contoso.msft	192.168.x
Stockholm	stockholm-dom.contoso.msft	192.168.x
Vienna	vienna-dom.contoso.msft	192.168.x
Moscow	moscow-dom.contoso.msft	192.168.x
NewDelhi	newdelhi-dom.contoso.msft	192.168.x
HongKong	hongkong-dom.contoso.msft	192.168.x
Tokyo	tokyo-dom.contoso.msft	192.168.x

Computer Name	Forward Lookup Zone	Network ID
Sydney	sydney-dom.contoso.msft	192.168.x
Melbourne	melbourne-dom.contoso.msft	192.168.x
Auckland	auckland-dom.contoso.msft	192.168.x
Manila	manila-dom.contoso.msft	192.168.x

▶ **To configure the DNS suffix for your computer**

Note Do not log on to the contoso domain to complete these steps. Log on to your local computer.

1. Log on to your local computer as Administrator with a password of **password**.
2. On the desktop, right-click the My Computer icon, and then click Properties.
3. In the System Properties dialog box, on the Network Identification tab, click the Properties button.
4. In the Identification Changes dialog box, click the More button.
5. In the DNS Suffix And NetBIOS Computer Name dialog box, in the Primary DNS Suffix Of This Computer text box, type *domain*.**contoso.msft** (where *domain* is your assigned domain name), and then click OK.
6. In the Identification Changes dialog box, click OK.
7. In the Network Identification message box, click OK.
8. In the System Properties dialog box, click OK.
9. In the System Settings Change message box, click the Yes button.

   The system restarts.

▶ **To install DNS on your server**

Note Do not log on to the contoso domain to complete these steps. Log on to your local computer.

1. Log on to your local computer as Administrator with a password of **password**.
2. Click Start, point to Settings, and then click Control Panel.
3. In the Control Panel window, double-click the Add/Remove Programs icon.
4. In the Add/Remove Programs dialog box, click the Add/Remove Windows Components button.

   The Windows Components Wizard starts.
5. In the Components list, select Networking Services, and then click the Details button.

6. In the Network Services dialog box, under the Subcomponents Of Networking Services list, select Domain Name System (DNS), and then click OK.

7. Click Next.

8. If prompted for the Windows 2000 Server distribution files, type **\\newyork\i386**.

   The appropriate files are copied.

9. Click the Finish button to complete the Windows Components Wizard.

10. Close the Add/Remove Programs dialog box.

11. Close the Control Panel window.

▶ **To create DNS forward and reverse lookup zones**

Note Do not log on to the contoso domain to complete these steps. Log on to your local computer.

---

1. Click Start, point to Programs, point to Administrative Tools, and then click DNS.

2. In the console tree, right-click the *Computer* node (where *Computer* is your assigned computer name), and then click Configure The Server.

3. Use the information provided in the following table to complete the Configure DNS Server Wizard. You should accept defaults when no information is specified.

Wizard Page	Do the Following
Forward Lookup Zone	Verify that the Yes, Create A Forward Lookup Zone option button is selected.
Zone Type	Verify that the Standard Primary option button is selected.
Zone Name	In the Name text box, type **domain.contoso.msft** (where *domain* is your assigned domain name).
Zone File	Verify that the Create A New File With This File Name option button is selected.
Reverse Lookup Zone	Verify that the Yes, Create A Reverse Lookup Zone option button is selected.
Zone Type	Verify that the Standard Primary option button is selected.
Reverse Lookup Zone	In the Network ID address box, type **192.168.x** (where x is your assigned classroom number).
Zone File	Verify that the Create A New File With This File Name option button is selected.

4. Close the wizard after it completes.

► **To configure DNS to support dynamic updates**

1. In the console tree, expand the *Computer* node (where *Computer* is your assigned computer name), expand the Forward Lookup Zones node, and then select the *Domain*.contoso.msft node (where *Domain* is your assigned domain name).

2. Right-click the *Domain*.contoso.msft node, and then click Properties.

3. In the *Domain*.contoso.msft Properties dialog box, in the Allow Dynamic Updates? drop-down list, select Yes, and then click OK.

4. In the console tree, expand the Reverse Lookup Zones node.

5. Right-click the 192.168.*y*.x Subnet node (where *y* is your assigned classroom number), and then click Properties.

6. In the 192.168.*y*.x Properties dialog box, in the Allow Dynamic Updates? drop-down list, select Yes, and then click OK.

7. Minimize the DNS console.

► **To configure TCP/IP to use your DNS server**

1. On the desktop, right-click the My Network Places icon, and then click Properties.

2. In the Network And Dial-up Connections window, right-click the Local Area Connection icon, and then click Properties.

3. In the Local Area Connection Properties dialog box, select Internet Protocol (TCP/IP), and then click the Properties button.

4. In the Internet Protocol (TCP/IP) Properties dialog box, in the Preferred DNS Server address box, type *IP_address* (where *IP_address* is your assigned IP address).

5. Click OK to close the Internet Protocol (TCP/IP) Properties dialog box.

6. Click OK to close the Local Area Connection Properties dialog box.

7. Close the Network And Dial-Up Connections window.

► **To dynamically register your server with DNS**

1. Click Start, and then click Run.

2. In the Open box, type **cmd**, and then click OK.

3. At the command prompt, type **ipconfig /registerdns**, and then press ENTER.

4. Close the Command Prompt window.

5. Maximize the DNS console.

6. In the console tree, select the 192.168.*y*.x Subnet node (where *y* is your assigned classroom number).

7. Press F5 to refresh the display.

Notice that a new pointer resource record appears in the Details pane.

8. Close all open windows.

Exercise 2
Installing Active Directory

In this exercise, you will install Active Directory on your stand-alone server.

▶ **To install Active Directory on your computer**

1. Click Start, and then click Run.

2. In the Open box, type **dcpromo.exe**. The Active Directory Installation Wizard starts.

Note If the Active Directory Installation Wizard does not start, then you may need to convert the C: drive to NTFS, click Start and then click Run, and type **convert c: /fs:ntfs** at the prompt and press ENTER. Reboot the computer and the drive will be converted to NTFS.

---

3. Use the information provided in the following table to complete the Active Directory Installation Wizard. You should accept defaults when no information is specified.

Wizard Page	Do the Following
Domain Controller Type	Select the Domain Controller For A New Domain option button.
Create Tree Or Child Domain	Verify that the Create A New Domain Tree option button is selected.
Create Or Join Forest	Verify that the Create A New Forest Of Domain Trees option button is selected.
New Domain Name	In the Full DNS Name For New Domain text box, type *domain*.**contoso.msft** (where *domain* is your assigned domain name).
NetBIOS Domain Name	Verify that *DOMAIN* appears.
Permissions	Select the Permissions Compatible Only With Windows 2000 Servers option button.
Directory Services Restore Mode Administrator Password	In both the Password and Confirm Password text boxes, type **password**.

4. When the wizard completes, click the Finish button.

   A dialog box appears, prompting you to restart the computer so that the changes you made can take effect.

5. Click the Restart Now button.

   The computer restarts.

Exercise 3
Verifying the Active Directory Installation

In this exercise, you will verify the Active Directory installation on your new domain controller.

▶ **To verify that the required service (SRV) resource records have been registered in DNS**

1. Log on to *domain* (where *domain* is your assigned domain name) as Administrator with a password of **password**.

2. Click Start, point to Programs, point to Administrative Tools, and then click DNS.

3. In the console tree, expand the *Computer* node (where *Computer* is your assigned computer name), and then expand the Forward Lookup Zones node.

4. Expand the *Domain*.contoso.msft node.

5. What folders appear below your domain name?

_____

_____

Note If the msdcs, _sites, _tcp, and _udp folders do not appear below the domain name, start and stop the netlogon service by using the net stop and net start commands. To start and stop the netlogon service, enter from the DOS prompt: **net stop netlogon** and then **net start netlogon**. Stopping and restarting the netlogon service will force the creation of the folders below the domain name.

6. Close the DNS console.

▶ **To verify that the shared system volume (SYSVOL) was created and shared**

1. Click Start, point to Programs, point to Administrative Tools, and then click Computer Management.

2. In the console tree, expand the System Tools node, expand the Shared Folders node, and then select the Shares node.

   In the Details pane, verify that SYSVOL appears in the list of shares.

3. Close the Computer Management console.

▶ **To verify that the Active Directory database files were created**

1. Click Start, and then click Run.

2. In the Open box, type **%systemroot%\ntds**, and then click OK.

3. In the NTDS window, click Tools, Folder Options.

4. In the Folder Options dialog box, click the View tab.

5. In the Advanced Settings box, clear the Hide File Extensions For Known File Types check box, and then click OK.

6. What folders and files appear in the NTDS window?

_____

_____

7. Close the NTDS window.

Exercise 4
Creating Organizational Unit Structures

In this exercise, you will create organizational units within your existing Active Directory structure.

Scenario

Contoso, Ltd., has three divisions that operate as separate business units: the research division, the manufacturing division, and the sales division. Each business unit must be able to administer its own accounts and resources.

In addition, at each location, a network administrator, who reports to the information technologies department at headquarters, must be able to administer all accounts and resources within his or her location.

As a result, you have been given the following organizational unit (OU) design that you must implement in your Active Directory domain.

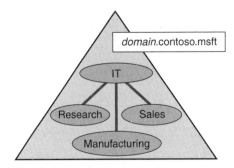

Figure 4.1 Organizational Unit Design for Contoso, Ltd.

▶   **To create the OUs for your Active Directory domain**

1. Click Start, point to Programs, point to Administrative Tools, and then click Active Directory Users And Computers.

2. In the console tree, expand and select the *Domain*.contoso.msft node, (where *Domain* is your assigned domain name).

3. In the details pane, examine the objects that are directly beneath the *Domain*.contoso.msft node. What are the objects that are created by default in your domain?

_____

_____

4. In the console tree, right-click the *Domain*.contoso.msft node, point to New, and then click Organizational Unit.

5. In the Name text box, type **IT**, and then click OK.

6. In the console tree, right-click the IT node, point to New, and then click Organizational Unit.

7. In the Name text box, type **Research**, and then click OK.

8. Repeat steps 6 and 7 for the Manufacturing and Sales OUs.

9. In the console tree, expand the IT node.

   Notice that the Manufacturing, Research, and Sales OUs are beneath the IT OU.

10. Close the Active Directory Users And Computers console.

Lab 5: DNS and Active Directory Integration

Objectives

After completing this lab, you will be able to

- Convert a standard primary DNS zone to an Active Directory integrated zone.
- Configure an Active Directory integrated zone to perform secured updates.
- Verify proper DNS operation by using the nslookup command.
- Verify proper DNS operation by using the DNS console.

Before You Begin

To complete this lab, you will need the information in the following table. Ask your instructor to supply you with the information.

When you are asked for	Use
Classroom number	
IP address	
Domain name	

Estimated time to complete this lab: 30 minutes

Exercise 1
Converting a Standard Primary DNS
Zone to an Active Directory Integrated Zone

In this exercise, you will convert an existing standard primary DNS zone to an Active Directory integrated zone.

▶   **To convert a standard primary zone to an Active Directory integrated zone**

1. Log on to *domain* (where *domain* is your assigned domain name) as Administrator with a password of **password**.

2. Click Start, point to Programs, point to Administrative Tools, and then click DNS.

3. In the console tree, expand the *Computer* node (where *Computer* is your assigned computer name), expand the Forward Lookup Zones node, and then select the *Domain*.contoso.msft node.

4. In the console tree, right-click the *Domain*.contoso.msft node, and then click Properties.

5. In the *Domain*.contoso.msft Properties dialog box, click the Change button.

6. In the Change Zone Type dialog box, select the Active Directory-Integrated option button, and then click OK.

7. In the DNS message box, click OK.

8. In the *Domain*.contoso.msft Properties dialog box, click OK.

9. In the console tree, expand the Reverse Lookup Zones node, and then select the 192.168.*y*.x Subnet node (where *y* is your assigned classroom number).

10. Right-click the 192.168.*y*.x Subnet node, and then click Properties.

11. In the 192.168.*y*.x Subnet Properties dialog box, click the Change button.

12. In the Change Zone Type dialog box, select the Active Directory-Integrated option button, and then click OK.

13. In the DNS message box, click OK.

14. In the 192.168.*y*.x Subnet Properties dialog box, click OK.

Exercise 2
Configure an Active Directory
Integrated Zone for Secured Updates

In this exercise, you will configure an Active Directory integrated zone on your server to allow only secured updates.

▶ **To configure an Active Directory integrated zone for secured updates**

1. In the console tree, expand the *Computer* node (where *Computer* is your assigned computer name), expand the Forward Lookup Zones node, and then select the *Domain*.contoso.msft node (where *Domain* is your assigned domain name).

2. Right-click the *Domain*.contoso.msft node, and then click Properties.

3. In the *Domain*.contoso.msft Properties dialog box, in the Allow Dynamic Updates? drop-down list, select Only Secure Updates, and then click OK.

4. In the console tree, expand the Reverse Lookup Zones node, and then select the 192.168.*y*.x Subnet node (where *y* is your assigned classroom number).

5. Right-click the 192.168.*y*.x Subnet node, and then click Properties.

6. In the 192.168.*y*.x Subnet Properties dialog box, in the Allow Dynamic Updates? drop-down list, select Only Secure Updates, and then click OK.

7. Close the DNS console.

Exercise 3
Verifying Proper DNS Operation
by Using the nslookup Command

In this exercise, you will verify the proper operation of your DNS server by using the nslookup command.

▶   **To verify proper DNS operation by using nslookup**

1. Click Start, and then click Run.

2. In the Open box, type **cmd**, and then click OK.

3. At the command prompt, type **nslookup** *computer.domain*.**contoso.msft** (where *computer* is your assigned computer name and *domain* is your assigned domain name), and then press ENTER.

   The DNS server responds by displaying the name and IP address of the DNS server, followed by the name and IP address of your computer.

4. At the command prompt, type **nslookup** *ip_address* (where *ip_address* is your assigned IP address), and then press ENTER.

   The DNS server responds by displaying the name and IP address of the DNS server, followed by the name and IP address of your computer.

5. Close the Command Prompt window.

Exercise 4
Verifying Proper DNS Operation
by Using the DNS Console

In this exercise, you will verify the proper operation of your DNS server by using the DNS console.

▶ **To verify proper DNS operation by using the DNS console**

1. Click Start, point to Programs, point to Administrative Tools, and then click DNS.

2. In the console tree, select the *Computer* node (where *Computer* is your assigned computer name). Right-click the *Computer* node, and then click Properties.

3. In the *Computer* Properties dialog box, on the Monitoring tab, select the A Simple Query Against This DNS Server check box, and then click the Test Now button.

   In the Test Results box, notice the success or failure of the query.

4. Select the A Recursive Query To Other DNS Servers check box, and then click the Test Now button.

   In the Test results box, notice the success or failure of the query.

5. Open the Logging tab.

   Notice the logging options that you can select to assist in troubleshooting DNS problems.

   When you enable DNS logging, where can you view the logging information?

   _____

   _____

   You can view the DNS logging information in Event Viewer under the DNS log.

6. Click the Cancel button.

7. Close the DNS console.

Lab 6: Configuring Active Directory Sites

Objectives

After completing this lab, you will be able to

- Create and configure a new site in an Active Directory structure.
- Create and configure subnets within an Active Directory site.
- Create and configure links between sites.
- Manage servers within a site.

Estimated time to complete this lab: 30 minutes

Scenario

Over the next few months, the human resources department of Contoso, Ltd., will conduct training for the Microsoft Windows 2000 deployment. In each city in which Contoso, Ltd., has a branch office, the company has obtained a training facility in a conference center or hotel as shown below. Approximately 30 to 40 employees of each branch office will attend training for three weeks.

You must provide access to the local Contoso, Ltd., location so that the students can be trained on Windows 2000 and Active Directory. You must create another site and install a domain controller at the training facility.

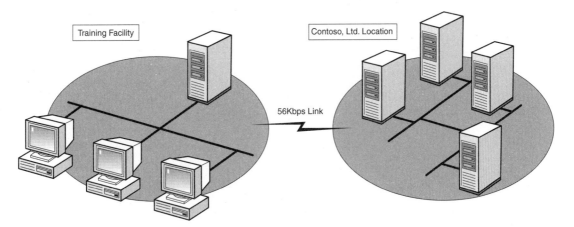

Figure 6.1 Contosco, Ltd. location and training facility

Exercise 1
Managing Active Directory Sites

In this exercise, you will create and configure an Active Directory site in your existing Active Directory domain.

▶ **To rename a site object in Active Directory**

1. Log on to *domain* (where *domain* is your assigned domain name) as **Administrator** with a password of **password**.

2. Click Start, point to Programs, point to Administrative Tools, and then click Active Directory Sites And Services.

3. In the console tree, select the Sites node; in the Details pane, right-click Default-First-Site-Name; and then click Rename.

4. Rename Default-First-Site-Name to *computer*-**Site** (where *computer* is your assigned computer name).

▶ **To create a new site object in Active Directory**

1. In the console tree, right-click the Sites folder, point to New, and then click Site.

2. In the New Object-Site dialog box, in the Name text box, type *computer*-**Training-Site** (where *computer* is your assigned computer name).

3. In the Link Name column, select DEFAULTIPSITELINK, and then click OK.

4. In the Active Directory message box, click OK.

Exercise 2
Managing Active Directory Subnets

In this exercise, you will create and configure Active Directory subnets and assign sites to each subnet within your existing Active Directory domain.

▶ **To create a subnet object in Active Directory**

1. In the console tree, expand the Sites node, select the Subnets node, right-click the Subnets node, point to New, and then click Subnet.

2. In the New Object-Subnet dialog box, in the Address box, type *ip_address* (where *ip_address* is your assigned IP address).

3. In the Mask box, type **255.255.255.0**.

4. In the Site Name list, select *Computer*-Site (where *Computer* is your assigned computer name), and then click OK.

5. In the console tree, right-click the Subnet folder, point to New, and then click Subnet.

6. In the New Object-Subnet dialog box, in the Address box, type **10.0.0.0**.

7. In the Mask box, type **255.255.255.192**.

8. In the Site Name list, select *Computer*-Training-Site, and then click OK.

Why would you want to create multiple Active Directory subnets within an Active Directory site?

_____

_____

Exercise 3
Manage Active Directory Site Links

In this exercise, you will create and configure Active Directory site links between sites in your existing Active Directory infrastructure.

▶ **To create a site link object in Active Directory**

1. In the console tree, expand the Inter-Site Transports node, select the IP node, right-click the IP node, and then click New Site Link.

2. In the New Object-Site Link dialog box, in the Name text box, type *computer*-**Training-Site-Link** (where *computer* is your assigned computer name).

3. Verify that *computer*-Site and *computer*-Training-Site are listed in the Sites In This Site Link list, and then click OK.

▶ **To configure inter-site replication in Active Directory**

1. In the console tree, expand the Inter-Site Transports node, select the IP node, and in the Details pane, right-click *Computer*-Training-Site-Link (where *Computer* is your assigned computer name), and then click Properties.

2. In the *Computer*-Training-Site-Link Properties dialog box, in the Cost box, type **200**.

3. In the Replicate Every box, type **1440**.

4. Click the Change Schedule button.

5. In the Schedule For *Computer*-Training-Site-Link dialog box, enable Active Directory replication to occur between 9 P.M. and 7 A.M., and then click OK.

6. In the *Computer*-Training-Site-Link Properties dialog box, click OK.

Exercise 4
Manage Servers Within Active Directory Sites

In this exercise, you will create and configure servers within sites in your existing Active Directory infrastructure.

▶ **To create a server object in Active Directory**

1. In the console tree, expand the *Computer*-Site node (where *Computer* is your assigned computer name), expand the Servers node, right-click the Servers node, point to New, and then click Server.

2. In the New Object-Server dialog box, in the Name text box, type ***computer-Training-Server***, and then click OK.

▶ **To move server objects between sites**

1. In the console tree, expand the *Computer*-Site node (where *Computer* is your assigned computer name), expand the Servers node, select the *Computer*-Training-Server node, right-click the *Computer*-Training-Server node, and then click Move.

2. In the Move Server dialog box, in the Site Name list, select *Computer*-Training-Site, and then click OK.

▶ **To enable a global catalog on a server**

1. In the console tree, expand the *Computer*-Site node (where *Computer* is your assigned computer name), expand the Servers node, expand the *Computer* node, right-click the NTDS Settings node, and then click Properties.

2. In the NTDS Settings Properties dialog box, verify that the Global Catalog check box is selected, and then click OK.

▶ **To remove an inoperative server from a site**

1. In the console tree, expand the *Computer*-Training-Site node (where *Computer* is your assigned computer name), expand the Servers node, right-click the *Computer*-Training-Server node, and then click Delete.

2. In the Active Directory message box, click the Yes button.

3. Close the Active Directory Sites And Services console.

Lab 7: User Account Administration

Objectives

After completing this lab, you will be able to

- Create new user accounts within an Active Directory organizational unit.
- Create multiple user accounts in a domain by using bulk import.
- Manage profiles and home directories for existing users.

Estimated time to complete this lab: 30 minutes

Exercise 1
Creating User Accounts

In this exercise, you will create and modify user accounts in your existing Active Directory domain.

▶ **To create a new user account in Active Directory**

1. Log on to *domain* as **Administrator** (where *domain* is your assigned domain name) with a password of **password**.

2. Click Start, point to Programs, point to Administrative Tools, and then click Active Directory Users And Computers.

3. In the console tree, expand the *Domain*.contoso.msft node, select the *Domain*.contoso.msft node, right-click the *Domain*.contoso.msft node, point to New, and then click Organizational Unit.

4. In the New Object-Organizational Unit dialog box, in the Name text box, type **Training Course**, and then click OK.

5. In the console tree, select the Training Course node, right-click the Training Course node, point to New, and then click User.

6. Complete the information in the New Object-User dialog box by using the information in the following table. Create a new user object for each user in the table and make them members of the Print Operators group.

First Name	Last Name	Logon Name	Password	Must Change Password
Don	Hall	donh	password	No
James	Smith	jamess	password	No
Jon	Morris	jonm	password	No

▶ **To modify existing users in Active Directory**

1. In the console tree, select the Training Course organizational unit.

2. In the Details pane, right-click Don Hall, and then click Properties.

3. In the Don Hall Properties dialog box, on the Account tab, click the Logon Hours button.

4. In the Logon Hours For Don Hall dialog box, permit the user to log on from Monday through Friday, between 7 A.M. and 7 P.M., and then click OK.

5. In the Don Hall Properties dialog box, on the Account tab, select the End Of option button, and then set the date to a year from today.

6. Click OK.

7. Complete Steps 2–6 for all the new user accounts.

Exercise 2
Creating Multiple User Accounts by Using Bulk Import

In this exercise, you will create multiple user accounts in your existing Active Directory domain by using bulk import.

▶ **To create an organizational unit to hold the new user accounts**

1. In the console tree, expand the *Domain*.contoso.msft node (where *Domain* is your assigned domain name), select the *Domain*.contoso.msft node, right-click the *Domain*.contoso.msft node, point to New, and then click Organizational Unit.

2. In the New Object-Organizational Unit dialog box, in the Name text box, type **contoso**, and then click OK.

3. Minimize the Active Directory Users And Computers console.

▶ **To create multiple user accounts by using bulk import**

1. Click Start, and then click Run.

2. In the Open box, type **c:\setup\newusers.txt**, and then click OK.

3. In the NewUsers-Notepad window, replace all occurrences of "domain" with your assigned domain name.

4. Save the edited file and close the NewUsers-Notepad window.

5. Click Start, and then click Run.

6. In the Open box, type **cmd**, and then click OK.

7. At the command prompt, type **c:**, and then press ENTER.

8. At the command prompt, type **cd setup**, and then press ENTER.

9. At the command prompt, type **csvde -?**, and then press ENTER.

   Review the -i and -f options in the usage statement.

10. At the command prompt, type **csvde -i -f newusers.txt**, and then press ENTER.

   The csvde utility reports that 22 entries were successfully modified.

11. At the command prompt, type **newpass**, and then press ENTER.

   The newpass script utility reports that passwords for the 22 new user accounts were successfully set.

12. Close the Command Prompt window.

▶   **To verify the user accounts added by using bulk import**

1. Maximize the Active Directory Users And Computers console.

2. In the console tree, expand the *Domain*.contoso.msft node (where *Domain* is your assigned domain name), select the Contoso node, right-click the Contoso node, and then click Refresh.

   In the Details pane, the list of users that you added by bulk import should appear. The list of users should match the list of users in the NewUsers.txt file.

3. Minimize the Active Directory Users And Computers console.

Exercise 3
Manage Profiles and Home Directories for Users

In this exercise, you will manage the profiles and home directories for the users that you added to your existing Active Directory infrastructure.

▶ **To create a shared folder to hold roaming user profiles and home directories**

1. Click Start, and then click Run.

2. In the Open box, type **c:**, and then click OK.

3. In the Local Disk (C:) window, right-click the right-hand pane, point to New, and then click Folder.

   A new folder named New Folder is created. The name is selected and ready for you to change.

4. Type **Profiles**, and then press ENTER.

5. Right-click the Profiles folder, and then click Properties.

6. In the Profiles Properties dialog box, on the Sharing tab, select the Share This Folder option button, and then click the Permissions button.

7. Verify that the Everyone group has full control (the Full Control, Change, and Read check boxes should be selected), and then click OK.

8. In the Profiles Properties dialog box, click OK.

9. Complete Steps 3–8 to create a folder called Users.

10. Close the Local Disk (C:) window.

▶ **To configure a user's home directory and roaming user profile**

1. Maximize the Active Directory Users And Computers console.

2. In the console tree, expand the *Domain*.contoso.msft node (where *Domain* is your assigned domain name), and then select the Training Course node.

3. In the Details pane, right-click Don Hall, and then click Properties.

4. In the Don Hall Properties dialog box, on the Profile tab, in the Profile Path text box, type **\\\computer\profiles\%username%** (where *computer* is your assigned computer name).

5. In the Connect drop-down list, select Y:.

6. In the To text box, type **\\\computer\users\%username%**, and then click OK.

7. Close the Active Directory Users And Computers console.

▶   **To test the user's home directory and roaming user profile**

1. Log off as Administrator.

2. Log on to *domain* (where *domain* is your assigned domain name) as **donh** with a password of **password**.

3. Right-click the desktop, and then click Properties.

4. In the Display Properties dialog box, on the Appearance tab, in the Scheme drop-down list, select Desert, and then click OK.

5. Log off as donh.

6. Log on to *domain* as **donh** with a password of **password**.

   Does the desktop color scheme match the Desert scheme?

   _____

   _____

7. Click Start, and then click Run.

8. In the Open box, type *computer***profiles** (where *computer* is your assigned computer name), and then click OK.

9. In the Profiles On *Computer* window, double-click the donh folder.

10. On the Tools menu, click Folder Options.

11. In the Folder Options dialog box, on the View tab, in the Advanced Settings list, select the Show Hidden Files And Folders option button, and then click the Like Current Folder button.

12. In the Folder Views message box, click the Yes button.

13. In the Folder Options dialog box, click OK.

    What folders and files appear in the window?

    _____

    _____

    _____

14. Close all open windows.

15. On the desktop, double-click the My Computer icon.

16. In the My Computer window, examine the list of connected resources and notice that Donh On '*Computer*\\Users' (Y:) is one of the connected network resources.

    Why did Microsoft Windows 2000 connect to that network resource?

    _____

    _____

17. Close the My Computer window.

Lab 8: Group Account Administration

Objectives

After completing this lab, you will be able to

- Create new group accounts within an Active Directory organizational unit.
- Nest global groups to assist in the administration of users.
- Manage membership for existing groups.
- Run applications as another user by using Run As.

Estimated time to complete this lab: 30 minutes

Exercise 1
Creating Group Accounts

In this exercise, you will create group accounts in your existing Active Directory domain.

▶   **To create new groups in Active Directory**

1. Log on to *domain* (where *domain* is your assigned domain name) as **Administrator** with a password of **password**.

2. Click Start, point to Programs, point to Administrative Tools, and then click Active Directory Users And Computers.

3. In the console tree, expand the *Domain*.contoso.msft node.

4. Select the IT node, right-click the IT node, point to New, and then click Group.

5. In the New Object–Group dialog box, in the Group Name text box, type **IT Department**.

6. Verify that the Global option button and the Security option button are selected, and then click OK.

7. In the console tree, expand the IT node.

8. Repeat steps 3–5 for each of the organizational units below the IT node. Use the group names given in the following table. In step 4, substitute the organizational unit in the table for the IT organizational unit, then create the group object under each organizational unit.

Organizational Unit	Group Name
Manufacturing	Manufacturing Department
Research	Research Department
Sales	Sales Department

9. In the console tree, select the IT node.

10. In the Details pane, double-click IT Department.

11. In the IT Department Properties dialog box, on the Members tab, click the Add button.

12. In the Select Users, Contacts, Or Computers dialog box, attempt to add the Manufacturing Department group to the IT Department group.

    Were you successful in adding the Manufacturing Department group to the IT Department group? Why or why not?

    _____

    _____

13. Close the Active Directory Users And Computers console.

Exercise 2
Nesting Group Accounts

In this exercise, you will convert your existing domain from mixed mode to native mode and then nest group accounts in your existing Active Directory domain.

▶ **To convert a domain from mixed mode to native mode**

1. Click Start, point to Programs, point to Administrative Tools, and then click Active Directory Domains And Trusts.

2. In the console tree, select the *Domain*.contoso.msft node (where *Domain* is your assigned domain name), right-click the *Domain*.contoso.msft node, and then click Properties.

3. In the *Domain*.Contoso.msft properties dialog box, click the Change Mode button.

4. In the Change Mode message box, click the Yes button.

5. In the *Domain*.Contoso.msft properties dialog box, click OK.

6. In the Active Directory message box, click OK.

7. Close the Active Directory Domains And Trusts console.

▶ **To modify the membership of the groups in Active Directory**

1. Click Start, point to Programs, point to Administrative Tools, and then click Active Directory Users And Computers.

2. In the console tree, expand the *Domain*.contoso.msft node (where *Domain* is your assigned domain name), expand the IT node, and then select the IT node.

3. In the Details pane, double-click IT Department.

4. In the IT Department Properties dialog box, on the Member Of tab, click the Add button.

5. In the Select Groups dialog box, in the Name column, click Manufacturing Department, and then click the Add button.

6. In the Name column, select Research Department, and then click the Add button.

7. In the Name column, select Sales Department, and then click the Add button.

8. Click OK.

9. In the IT Department Properties dialog box, click OK.

Exercise 3
Managing Group Membership

In this exercise, you will manage the membership of group accounts in your existing Active Directory domain.

▶ **To manage group membership in Active Directory**

1. In the console tree, expand the *Domain*.contoso.msft node (where *Domain* is your assigned domain name), select the IT node, right-click the IT node, and then click Move.

2. In the Move dialog box, click Contoso, and then click OK.

3. In the console tree, select the Contoso node.

4. On the View menu, click Choose Columns.

5. In the Modify Columns dialog box, in the Hidden Columns list, select Department, click the Add button, and then click OK.

    The department column appears in the Details pane.

6. In the console tree, select the Contoso node.

7. In the Details pane, click the Department column heading.

    The users are sorted by department name.

8. In the Details pane, select the first user in the IT Department, hold down the SHIFT key, and then click the last user in the IT Department.

    All the users in the IT Department are selected.

9. Right-click the selected users, and then click Add Members To A Group.

10. In the Select Group dialog box, in the Name list, select IT Department, and then click OK.

11. Click OK on the Active Directory dialog box.

12. Right-click the selected users, and then click Move.

13. In the Move dialog box, expand the Contoso node, select the IT node, and then click OK.

14. Use the information in the following table to complete steps 8–12 for each of the departments so that the users are added to the appropriate groups and moved to the proper organizational units.

Add users in this department	To this group	Move to this OU
Manufacturing	Manufacturing Department	Manufacturing
Research	Research Department	Research
Sales	Sales Department	Sales

15. Close the Active Directory Users And Computers console.

Exercise 4
Running Applications As Another User

In this exercise, you will log on as donh and then run applications as the Administrator account in your existing Active Directory domain.

▶ **To verify that a user cannot create an organizational unit**

1. Log off as Administrator.

2. Log on to *domain* (where *domain* is your assigned domain name) as **donh** with a password of **password**.

3. Click Start, point to Programs, point to Administrative Tools, and then click Active Directory Users And Computers.

4. Attempt to create an organizational unit named **Training Lab** under the *Domain*.contoso.msft node.

   Were you able to create the organizational unit? Why or why not?

   _____

   _____

5. Close the Active Directory Users And Computers console.

▶ **To create an organizational unit as a user by using Run As**

1. Click Start, point to Programs, point to Administrative Tools, and point to (but do not click) Active Directory Users And Computers.

2. Press the SHIFT key and simultaneously right-click Active Directory Users And Computers, and then click Run As.

3. In the Run As Other User dialog box, select the Run The Program As The Following User option button.

4. In the User Name text box, verify that Administrator appears.

5. In the Password text box, type **password**.

6. In the Domain text box, type *domain* (where *domain* is your assigned domain name), and then click OK.

7. In the console tree, expand the *Domain*.contoso.msft node, select the *Domain*.Contoso.msft node, right-click the *Domain*.contoso.msft node, point to New, and then click Organizational Unit.

   You should be able to create the organizational unit, but do not create the organizational unit at this time.

8. Click the Cancel button.

9. Close the Active Directory Users And Computers console.

Lab 9: Securing Disk Resources

Objectives

After completing this lab, you will be able to

- Assign NTFS file and folder permissions to users and groups.

- Evaluate NTFS file and folder permissions.

- Assign special NTFS file and folder permissions so that users can take owner-ship of files and folders.

- Evaluate NTFS file and folder permissions when users move files or folders.

Before You Begin

To complete this lab, you need the following:

- User accounts created in Lab 7.

- Group accounts created in Lab 8.

Users and Groups Used in This Lab

The following table lists the users and groups that are used in this lab's exercises. Refer to the table when you need to determine the user name, password, or group membership.

User	User Name	Password	Group Membership
John Saunders	johns	password	IT Department
Phil Thompson	philt	password	Manufacturing Department
Lori Cook	loric	password	Research Department

Tip Remember that the IT Department group is a member of the Manufacturing Department and Research Department groups.

Estimated time to complete this lab: 45 minutes

Exercise 1
Assigning NTFS File and Folder Permissions

In this exercise, you will assign NTFS file and folder permissions to the user and group accounts in your Active Directory domain.

▶ **To create the folders and files that you will secure**

1. Log on to *domain* (where *domain* is your assigned domain name) as **Administrator** with a password of **password**.

2. Click Start, and then click Run.

3. In the Open box, type **c:**, and then click OK.

4. In the Local Disk (C:) window, create the directory structure depicted in the following diagram.

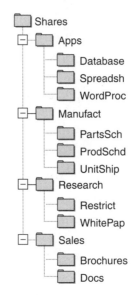

Figure 9.1 Directory structure

▶ **To assign NTFS permissions to the folders and files that you created**

1. If the directory tree doesn't already appear in the left-hand pane of the Local Disk (C:) window, click the Folders button in the toolbar.

2. In the directory tree, select the Shares node.

3. In the right-hand pane, right-click the Apps folder, and then click Properties.

4. In the Apps Properties dialog box, on the Security tab, clear the Allow Inheritable Permissions From Parent To Propagate To This Object check box.

5. In the Security message box, click the Remove button.

6. In the Apps Properties dialog box, on the Security tab, click the Add button.

7. In the Select Users, Computers, Or Groups dialog box, in the Name list, select Everyone, and then click the Add button.

8. In the Name list, select Administrators, click the Add button, and then click OK.

9. In the Apps Properties dialog box, on the Security tab, select Everyone, and then clear all check boxes in the Allow column except the Read check box.

10. Select Administrators, select the Full Control check box in the Allow column, and then click OK.

11. Create the files specified in the following table.

In This Folder	Create This File	That is This Type
C:\Shares\Manufact\ProdSchd	1st-Qtr	Text document
C:\Shares\Manufact\ProdSchd	2nd-Qtr	Text document
C:\Shares\Manufact\ProdSchd	3rd-Qtr	Text document
C:\Shares\Research\Restrict	NewProducts	Text document
C:\Shares\Sales\Brochures	Products	WordPad document

12. Assign NTFS permissions as specified in the following table.

To These Files	Assign These Permissions
1st-Qtr	Everyone: Read Manufacturing Department: Full Control
2nd-Qtr	Everyone: Read Manufacturing Department: Full Control
3rd-Qtr	Everyone: all *but* Full Control Manufacturing Department: Full Control
NewProducts	Everyone: Read Research Department: Full Control
Products	Everyone: Read Sales Department: Full Control

Tip To assign the permissions in the previous table, you need to clear the Allow Inheritable Permissions check box to remove any existing permissions.

Tip To assign the permissions in the previous table, you need to clear the Allow Inheritable Permissions check box to remove any existing permissions.

13. Assign NTFS permissions as specified in the following table.

To These Folders	Assign These Permissions
Apps Apps\Database Apps\SpreadSh Apps\WordProc	Everyone: Read IT Department: Full Control Administrators: Full Control
Manufact Manufact\PartsSch Manufact\ProdSchd Manufact\UnitShip	Everyone: Read Manufacturing Department: Full Control Administrators: Full Control
Research Research\WhitePap Research\Restrict	Everyone: Read Research Department: Full Control Administrators: Full Control Research Department: Full Control
Sales Sales\Brochures Sales\Docs	Everyone: Read Sales Department: Full Control Administrators: Full Control

14. Close all open windows.

Exercise 2
Evaluating NTFS File and Folder Permissions

In this exercise, you will evaluate the NTFS file and folder permissions that you assigned to the users and groups in your Active Directory domain.

▶ **To evaluate NTFS file and folder permissions as Administrator**

1. On the desktop, right-click the My Computer icon, and then click Explore.

2. In the My Computer window, in the left-hand pane, expand the Local Disk (C:) node, expand the Shares node, expand the Apps node, and then select the Database node.

3. Right-click in the right-hand pane, point to New, and then click Text Document. Name the new text document **ReadMe.txt**.

   Were you successful in creating a file in the directory? Why or why not?

   _____

   _____

4. In the right-hand pane, right-click the ReadMe file, and then click Delete.

   Were you successful in deleting the file in the directory? Why or why not?

   _____

   _____

5. In the left-hand pane, navigate to the C:\Shares\Manufact\ProdSchd node, and then select the ProdSchd node.

6. In the right-hand pane, double-click the 1st-Qtr file.

7. In the 1st-Qtr–Notepad window, modify the contents of the text file.

8. On the File menu, click the Save button.

   Were you successful in modifying 1st-Qtr? Why or why not?

   _____

   _____

9. Repeat Steps 6–8 for the 3rd-Qtr file in the ProdSchd folder.

   Were you successful in modifying 3rd-Qtr? Why or why not?

   _____

   _____

10. In the left-hand pane, navigate to D:\Shares\Research\Restrict, and then click Restrict.

Were you successful in viewing the contents of the Restrict folder? Why or why not?

_____

_____

11. Close all open windows.

▶ **To evaluate NTFS file and folder permissions as John Saunders**

1. Log off as Administrator.

2. Log on to *domain* (where *domain* is your assigned domain name) as **johns** with a password of **password**.

3. Use the same steps that you completed for the Administrator account, in the previous procedure, to evaluate the NTFS file and folder permissions for the user.

In the following table, record the success or failure of each task and the reason why you were or were not able to perform the task.

Task	Success	Why or Why Not?
Create a file called ReadMe in the C:\Shares\Apps\Database folder.		
Delete the file called ReadMe in the C:\Shares\Apps\Database folder.		
Modify the 1st-Qtr file in the C:\Shares\Manufact\ProdSchd folder.		
Modify the 3rd-Qtr file in the C:\Shares\Manufact\ProdSchd folder.		
Modify the NewProducts file in the C:\Shares\Research\Restrict folder.		
View the contents of the C:\Shares\Research\Restrict folder.		
Modify the Products file in the C:\Shares\Sales\Brochures folder.		

How did the permissions assigned John Saunders differ from the permissions assigned to the Administrators group?

_____

_____

▶ **To evaluate NTFS file and folder permissions as Phil Thompson**

1. Log off as johns.

2. Log on to *domain* (where *domain* is your assigned domain name) as **philt** with a password of **password**.

3. Use the same steps that you completed for the Administrator account to evaluate the NTFS file and folder permissions for the user.

   In the following table, record the success or failure of each task and the reason why you were or were not able to perform the task.

Task	Success	Why or Why Not?
Create a file called ReadMe in the C:\Shares\Apps\Database folder.		
Delete the file called ReadMe in the C:\Shares\Apps\Database folder.		
Modify the 1st-Qtr file in the C:\Shares\Manufact\ProdSchd folder.		
Modify the 3rd-Qtr file in the C:\Shares\Manufact\ProdSchd folder.		
View the contents of the C:\Shares\Research\Restrict folder.		
Modify the NewProducts file in the C:\Shares\Research\Restrict folder.		
Modify the Products file in the C:\Shares\Sales\Brochures folder.		

How do the permissions assigned to Phil Thompson differ from the previous users' permissions?

_____

_____

_____

▶ **To evaluate NTFS file and folder permissions as Lori Cook**

1. Log off as philt.

2. Log on to *domain* (where *domain* is your assigned domain name) as **loric** with a password of **password**.

3. Use the same steps that you completed for the Administrator account to evaluate the NTFS file and folder permissions for the user.

   In the following table, record the success or failure of each task and the reason why you were or were not able to perform the task.

Task	Success	Why or Why Not?
Create a file called ReadMe in the C:\Shares\Apps\Database folder.		
Delete the file called ReadMe in the C:\Shares\Apps\Database folder.		
Modify the 1st-Qtr file in the C:\Shares\Manufact\ProdSchd folder.		
Modify the 3rd-Qtr file in the C:\Shares\Manufact\ProdSchd folder.		
View the contents of the C:\Shares\Research\Restrict folder.		
Modify the NewProducts file in the C:\Shares\Research\Restrict folder.		
Modify the Products file in the C:\Shares\Sales\Brochures folder.		

How did the permissions assigned to Lori Cook differ from the previous users' permissions?

_____

_____

_____

_____

Exercise 3
Taking Ownership of Files and Folders

In this exercise, you will assign special permissions to a group so that a member of the group can take ownership of files and folders.

▶ **To assign special permissions to a group**

1. Log on to *domain* (where *domain* is your assigned domain name) as **Administrator** with a password of **password**.

2. On the desktop, right-click the My Computer icon, and then click Explore.

3. In the My Computer window, in the left-hand pane, navigate to the C:\Shares\Manufact\ProdSchd node, and then select the ProdSchd node.

4. In the right-hand pane, right-click the 2nd-Qtr file, and then click Properties.

5. In the 2nd-Qtr Properties dialog box, on the Security tab, click the Advanced button.

6. In the Access Control Settings For 2nd-Qtr dialog box, on the Owner tab, note the current owner of the file.

   Record the current owner of the 2nd-Qtr file in the space provided below.

   _____

7. Click the Cancel button.

8. In the 2nd-Qtr Properties dialog box, on the Security tab, select Manufacturing Department, select the Full Control check box, and then click OK.

▶ **To take ownership of a file**

1. Log off as Administrator.

2. Log on to *domain* (where *domain* is your assigned domain name) as **philt** with a password of **password**.

3. On the desktop, right-click the My Computer icon, and then click Explore.

4. In the My Computer window, in the left-hand pane, navigate to the C:\Shares\Manufact\ProdSchd node, and then select the ProdSchd folder.

5. In the right-hand pane, right-click the 2nd-Qtr file, and then click Properties.

6. In the 2nd-Qtr Properties dialog box, on the Security tab, click the Advanced button.

7. In the Access Control Settings For 2nd-Qtr dialog box, on the Owner tab, in the Change Owner To list, select Phil Thompson, and then click OK.

8. In the 2nd-Qtr Properties dialog box, on the Security tab, click the Advanced button.

9. In the Access Control Settings For 2nd-Qtr dialog box, on the Owner tab, note the current owner of the file.

Record the current owner of the 2nd-Qtr file in the space provided below.

_____

10. Click the Cancel button.

11. In the 2nd-Qtr Properties dialog box, click the Cancel button.

12. Close all open windows.

Exercise 4
Copying and Moving Files and Folders

In this exercise, you will evaluate the effect of copying or moving files and folders on NTFS permissions.

▶ **To evaluate NTFS permissions when you copy files and folders**

1. Log on to *domain* (where *domain* is your assigned domain name) as **Administrator** with a password of **password**.

2. On the desktop, right-click the My Computer icon, and then click Explore.

3. In the My Computer window, in the left-hand pane, navigate to the C:\Shares\Sales\Brochures node, and then select the Brochures node.

4. In the right-hand pane, right-click the Products file, and then click Properties.

5. In the Products Properties dialog box, on the Security tab, note the NTFS permissions assigned to the file.

   Record the NTFS permissions for the Products file in the space provided below.

   _____

   _____

6. Click the Cancel button.

7. In the right-hand pane, right-click the Products file, and then click Copy.

8. In the left-hand pane, navigate to the C:\Shares\Research\WhitePap node, and then select the WhitePap node.

9. Right-click in the right-hand pane, and then click Paste.

   The Products file appears in the right-hand pane.

10. In the right-hand pane, right-click the Products file, and then click Properties.

11. In the Products Properties dialog box, on the Security tab, note the NTFS permissions assigned to the file.

    How do the NTFS permissions assigned to the Products file compare to the NTFS permissions assigned to the original Products file?

    _____

    _____

▶ **To evaluate NTFS permissions when you move files and folders**

1. In the left-hand pane, navigate to the C:\Shares\Research\WhitePap node, and then select the WhitePap node.

2. In the right-hand pane, right-click the Products file, and then click Cut.

3. In the left-hand pane, navigate to the C:\Shares\Sales\Docs folder, and then select the Docs folder.

4. Right-click in the right-hand pane, and then click Paste.

   The Products file appears in the right-hand pane.

5. In the right-hand pane, right-click the Products file, and then click Properties.

6. In the Products Properties dialog box, on the Security tab, note the NTFS permissions assigned to the file.

   How do the NTFS permissions assigned to the Products file compare to the NTFS permissions assigned to the original Products file?

   _____

   _____

Lab 10: Sharing Disk Resources

Objectives

After completing this lab, you will be able to

- Share folders and assign shared folder permissions to users and groups.
- Evaluate the combination of the NTFS permissions and shared folder permissions.
- Configure Dfs to gain access to network resources.

Before You Begin

To complete this lab, you need the following:

- The user accounts created in Lab 7.
- The group accounts created in Lab 8.
- The files and folders with the appropriate NTFS permissions created in Lab 9.

Users and Groups Used in This Lab

The following table lists the users and groups that are used in this lab's exercises. Refer to the table when you need to determine the user name, password, or group membership.

User	User Name	Password	Group Membership
John Saunders	johns	password	IT Department
Phil Thompson	philt	password	Manufacturing Department
Louis Penna	louisp	password	Sales Department
Lori Cook	loric	password	Research Department

Tip Remember that the IT Department group is a member of the Manufacturing Department, Sales Department, and Research Department groups.

Estimated time to complete this lab: 45 minutes

Exercise 1
Sharing Folders and Assigning Shared Folder Permissions

In this exercise, you will share folders and then assign shared folder permissions to the user and group accounts in your Active Directory domain.

▶ **To share a folder and assign shared folder permissions**

1. Log on to *domain* (where *domain* is your assigned domain name) as **Administrator** with a password of **password**.

2. On the desktop, right-click the My Computer icon, and then click Explore.

3. In the My Computer dialog box, in the left-hand pane, expand the Local Disk (C:) node, expand the Shares node, and then select the Apps node.

4. In the left-hand pane, right-click the Apps node, and then click Sharing.

5. In the Apps Properties dialog box, select the Share This Folder option button, and then click the Permissions button.

6. In the Permissions For Apps dialog box, in the Permissions list, clear all check boxes except for the Allow check box in the Read row.

   The permissions for the Everyone group should be set to Read.

7. In the Permissions For Apps dialog box, click the Add button.

8. In the Select Users, Computer, Or Groups dialog box, select Administrators, click the Add button, and then click OK.

9. In the Permissions For Apps dialog box, in the Permissions list, select the Allow check box in the Full Control row, and then click OK.

10. In the Apps Properties dialog box, click OK.

11. Create the remaining shares based on the information in the following table.

Share This Folder	As	With These Permissions
C:\Shares\Manufact	Manufact	Everyone: Read Manufacturing Department: all *but* Full Control
C:\Shares\Research	Research	Everyone: Read Research Department: all *but* Full Control
C:\Shares\Sales	Sales	Everyone: Read Administrators: Full Control Sales Department: all *but* Full Control

12. Close all open windows.

Exercise 2
Evaluating Shared Folder
Permissions and NTFS Permissions

In this exercise, you will evaluate shared folder permissions and NTFS permissions.

▶ **To evaluate shared folder and NTFS permissions as Administrator**

1. Click Start, and then click Run.

2. In the Open box, type *computer***apps** (where *computer* is your assigned computer name), and then click OK.

3. In the Apps On *Computer* window, double-click Database.

4. Right-click in the window, point to New, and then click Text Document. Name the new text document **NewFile**.

   Were you successful in creating a file in the directory? Why or why not?

   _____

   _____

5. Right-click the NewFile icon, and then click Delete.

   Were you successful in deleting the file in the directory? Why or why not?

   _____

   _____

6. Close all open windows.

7. Click Start, and then click Run.

8. In the Open box, type *computer***manufact**, and then click OK.

9. In the Manufact On *Computer* window, double-click the ProdSchd folder.

10. Double-click the 2nd-Qtr file.

11. In the 2nd-Qtr–Notepad window, modify the contents of the text file.

12. On the File menu, click Save.

    Were you successful in modifying 2nd-Qtr? Why or why not?

    _____

    _____

13. Repeat steps 10–12 for the 3rd-Qtr file in the ProdSchd folder.

Were you successful in modifying 3rd-Qtr? Why or why not?

_____

_____

14. Close all open windows.

15. Click Start, and then click Run.

16. In the Open box, type *computer***research**, and then click OK.

17. In the Research On *Computer* window, double-click the Restrict folder.

Were you successful in viewing the contents of the Restrict folder? Why or why not?

_____

_____

18. Close all open windows.

How would you change the shared folder permissions so that the Administrators can properly administer the shared folders, if any changes are necessary?

_____

_____

▶   **To evaluate shared folder and NTFS permissions as John Saunders**

1. Log off as Administrator.

2. Log on to *domain* (where *domain* is your assigned domain name) as **johns** with a blank password.

3. Use the same steps that you completed for the Administrator account, in the previous procedure, to evaluate the shared folder and NTFS permissions for the user.

In the following table, record the success or failure of each task (where *Computer* is your assigned computer name) and the reason why you were or were not able to perform the task.

Task	Success	Why or why not?
Create a file called NewFile in the *Computer*\Apps\Database folder.		
Delete the file called NewFile in the *Computer*\Apps\Database folder.		
Modify the 2nd-Qtr file in the *Computer*\Manufact\ProdSchd folder.		
Modify the 3rd-Qtr file in the *Computer*\Manufact\ProdSchd folder.		
View the contents of the *Computer*\Research\Restrict folder.		
Modify the NewProducts file in the *Computer*\Research\Restrict folder.		
Modify the Products file in the *Computer*\Sales\Brochures folder.		

In Lab 9, you evaluated John Saunders' access from the local computer to resources on the local computer. How did John Saunders' access to resources change when he accessed the resources through the shared folders?

_____

_____

_____

How would you change the shared folder permissions to allow the IT Department to remotely administer the Apps folder?

_____

_____

4. Log off as johns.

▶   **To evaluate shared folder and NTFS permissions for the other users**

1. Using the information you have gained while accessing the shared folders as Administrator and John Saunders, predict the success or failure of the remaining users if they attempt to perform the same tasks.

2. In the following table, predict the success or failure of each task (where *Computer* is your assigned computer name) and the reason why the user would or would not be able to perform the task.

Tip For those actions that you are uncertain about, log on as the user in question and attempt to perform the action.

Task	Phil Thompson	Louis Penna	Lori Cook
Create a file called NewFile in the *Computer*\Apps\Database folder.			
Delete the file called NewFile in the *Computer*\Apps\Database folder.			
Modify the 2nd-Qtr file in the *Computer*\Manufact\ProdSchd folder.			
Modify the 3rd-Qtr file in the *Computer*\Manufact\ProdSchd folder.			
View the contents of the *Computer*\Research\Restrict folder.			
Modify the NewProducts file in the *Computer*\Research\Restrict folder.			
Modify the Products file in the *Computer*\Sales\Brochures folder.			

What restrictions were imposed by the shared folder permissions that would not have been imposed by the NTFS permissions alone?

_____

_____

_____

What are some tasks that the users would not be able to perform through the shared folders?

_____

_____

_____

_____

How could you change the shared folder permissions to accomplish the tasks from the previous question?

_____

_____

_____

_____

Exercise 3
Configuring Dfs to Provide Access to Distributed Shared Folders

In this exercise, you will configure Dfs to provide access to shared folders that are distributed between two servers.

▶ **To create the Dfs root**

1. Log on to *domain* (where *domain* is your assigned domain name) as **Administrator** with a password of **password**.

2. Click Start, and then click Run.

3. In the Open box, type **c:**, and then click OK.

4. In the Local Disk (C:) window, right-click in the right-hand pane, point to New, and then click Folder. Name the new folder **DfsRoot**.

5. Close the Local Disk (C:) window.

6. Click Start, point to Programs, point to Administrative Tools, and then click Distributed File System.

7. In the Distributed File System console, on the Action menu, click New Dfs Root.

    The New Dfs Root Wizard starts.

8. Use the information provided in the following table to complete the New Dfs Root Wizard. You should accept defaults when no information is specified.

Wizard Page	Do the Following
Select The Dfs Root Type	Select the Create A Standalone Dfs Root option button.
Specify The Dfs Root Share	Select the Create A New Share option button. In the Path To Share text box, type **c:\dfsroot**. In the Share name text box, type **DfsShares**.
Name The Dfs Root	In the Comment text box, type **Dfs root for all shared resources**.

9. When the wizard completes, click the Finish button.

▶ **To create Dfs links**

1. In the console tree, select the *Computer*\DfsShares node (where *Computer* is your assigned computer name), right-click the *Computer*\DfsShares node, and then click New Dfs Link.

2. In the Create A New Dfs Link dialog box, in the Link Name text box, type **DfsManufact**.

3. In the Send The User To This Shared Folder text box, type *computer* **manufact**.

4. In the Comment text box, type **Manufact Dfs Folder**, and then click OK.

5. In the console tree, right-click the DfsManufact node, and then click New Replica.

6. In the Add A New Replica dialog box, in the Send The User To This Shared Folder text box, type *your_partner's_computer***manufact** (where *your_partner's_computer* is the assigned name of your partner's computer), and then click OK.

▶ **To view the contents of a Dfs shared folder**

1. Click Start, and then click Run.

2. In the Open box, type **c:\\shares\\manufact\\unitship**, and then click OK.

3. In the UnitShip window, right-click in the right-hand pane, point to New, and then click Text Document. Name the new text document *Computer* (where *Computer* is your assigned computer name).

4. Close the UnitShip window.

5. Click Start, and then click Run.

6. In the Open box, type *computer***dfsshares\\dfsmanufact\\unitship**, and then click OK.

The UnitShip window appears.

What is the name of the text document that appears in the UnitShip window?

_____

Did your partner see a text document of the same name? If not, how could you make the Dfs share display the same information?

_____

_____

Can you use File Replication Service (FRS) to replicate the folders' contents? If not, how could you replicate the folders' information?

_____

_____

_____

7. Close all open windows.

Lab 11: Administering Active Directory

Objectives

After completing this lab, you will be able to

- Publish network resources in Active Directory.
- Locate objects in Active Directory.
- Delegate administration of Active Directory.
- Back up and restore Active Directory.

Before You Begin

To complete this lab, you need the following:

- The user accounts created in Lab 7.
- The group accounts created in Lab 8.
- The files and folders with the appropriate NTFS permissions created in Lab 9.
- The shared folders with the appropriate permissions created in Lab 10.

Users and Groups Used in This Lab

The following table lists the users and groups that are used in this lab's exercises. Refer to the table when you need to determine the user name, password, or group membership.

User	User Name	Password	Group Membership
John Saunders	johns	password	IT Department
Phil Thompson	philt	password	Manufacturing Department
Lori Cook	loric	password	Research Department
Louis Penna	louisp	password	Sales Department

Tip Remember that the IT Department group is a member of the Manufacturing Department, Sales Department, and Research Department groups.

Estimated time to complete this lab: 45 minutes

Exercise 1
Publishing Network Resources in Active Directory

In this exercise, you will publish a printer and shared folders in Active Directory.

▶ **To create and share a printer**

1. Log on to *domain* (where *domain* is your assigned domain name) as **Administrator** with a password of **password**.

2. Click Start, point to Settings, and then click Printers.

3. In the Printers window, double-click Add Printer.

   The Add Printer Wizard starts.

4. Use the information provided in the following table to complete the Add Printer Wizard. You should accept defaults when no information is specified.

Wizard Page	Do the Following
Local Or Network Printer	Clear the Automatically Detect And Install My Plug And Play Printer check box.
Select The Printer Port	Select LPT2:.
Add Printer Wizard	In the Manufacturers list, select HP. In the Printers list, select HP LaserJet 4.
Location And Comment	In the Location text box, type *computer* **Printer** (where *computer* is your assigned computer name). In the Comment text box, type **Printer located in the central office**.
Print Test Page	Select the No option button.

5. When the wizard completes, click the Finish button.

6. Close all open windows.

▶ **To publish shared folders in Active Directory**

1. Click Start, point to Programs, point to Administrative Tools, and then click Active Directory Users And Computers.

2. In the console tree, right-click the *Domain*.contoso.msft node (where *Domain* is your assigned domain name), point to New, and then click Organizational Unit.

3. In the New Object–Organizational Unit dialog box, type *Domain* **Shared Folders**, and then click OK.

4. In the console tree, select the *Domain* Shared Folders node, right-click the *Domain* Shared Folders node, point to New, and then click Shared Folder.

5. In the New Object–Shared Folder dialog box, in the Name text box, type **Manufacturing Shared Folder–***computer* (where *computer* is your assigned computer name).

6. In the Network Path (\\Server\Share) text box, type ***computer*\Manufct**, and then click OK.

7. In the Details pane, right-click Manufacturing Shared Folder–*Computer*, and then click Properties.

8. In the Manufacturing Shared Folder–*Computer* Properties dialog box, click the Keywords button.

9. In the Keywords dialog box, type *computer*, and then click the Add button.

10. In the Keywords dialog box, type **Manufacturing**, click the Add button, and then click OK.

11. In the Manufacturing Shared Folder–*Computer* Properties dialog box, click OK.

12. In the console tree, select the *Domain* Shared Folders node, right-click the *Domain* Shared Folders node, point to New, and then click Shared Folder.

13. In the New Object–Shared Folder dialog box, in the Name text box, type **Manufacturing Shared Folder–***your_partner's_computer* (where *your_partner's_computer* is your partner's assigned computer name).

14. In the Network Path (\\Server\Share) text box, type ***your_partner's_computer* \Manufct**, and then click OK.

15. In the Details pane, right-click Manufacturing Shared Folder–*Your_Partner's_Computer*, and then click Properties.

16. In the Manufacturing Shared Folder–*Your_Partner's_Computer* Properties dialog box, click the Keywords button.

17. In the Keywords dialog box, type *your_partner's_computer*, and then click the Add button.

18. In the Keywords dialog box, type **manufacturing**, click the Add button, and then click OK.

19. In the Manufacturing Shared Folder–*Computer* Properties dialog box, click OK.

20. Close all open windows.

Exercise 2
Locating Objects in Active Directory

In this exercise, you will locate users, printers, and shared folders in your Active Directory domain.

▶ **To locate Active Directory users by using the Active Directory Users And Computers console**

1. Log on to *domain* (where *domain* is your assigned domain name) as **Administrator** with a password of **password**.

2. Click Start, point to Programs, point to Administrative Tools, and then click Active Directory Users And Computers.

3. In the console tree, right-click the *Domain*.contoso.msft node, and then click Find.

4. In the Find Users, Contacts, And Groups dialog box, in the Find drop-down list, select Custom Search.

5. In the Find Custom Search dialog box, on the Custom Search tab, click Field, point to User, and then click Name.

6. In the Value text box, type **S**, and then click the Add button.

7. Click the Find Now button.

   Which user(s) were returned in your search?

   _____

   _____

8. Click the Clear All button.

9. In the Find In The Directory message box, click OK.

10. In the Find Custom Search dialog box, on the Custom Search tab, click Field, point to User, and then click Telephone Number.

11. In the Value text box, type **555-1112**, and then click the Add button.

12. Click the Find Now button.

    Which user(s) were returned in your search?

    _____

    _____

▶ **To locate Active Directory users by using Search Assistant**

1. Click Start, point to Search, and then click For People.

2. In the Find People dialog box, in the Look In drop-down list, select Active Directory.

3. On the Advanced tab, under Define Criteria, select Name, select Starts With, and then type **S**.

4. Click the Add button, and then click the Find Now button.

Which user(s) were returned in your search?

_____

_____

What is the difference between the user(s) returned in this search and the user(s) returned in the search performed in Active Directory Users And Computers?

_____

_____

5. Close all open windows.

▶ **To locate printers in Active Directory by using Search Assistant**

1. Click Start, point to Search, and then click For Printers.

2. In the Find Printers dialog box, on the Printers tab, in the Location text box, type ***computer*** (where *computer* is your assigned computer name), and then click the Find Now button.

Which printer(s) were returned in your search?

_____

_____

3. Close all open windows.

▶ **To locate printers in Active Directory by using Active Directory Users And Computers**

1. Click Start, point to Programs, point to Administrative Tools, and then click Active Directory Users And Computers.

2. In the console tree, right-click the *Domain*.contoso.msft node (where *Domain* is your assigned domain name), and then click Find.

3. In the Find Users, Contacts, And Groups dialog box, in the Find drop-down list, select Printers.

4. In the Location text box, type ***computer*** (where *computer* is your assigned computer name), and then click the Find Now button.

Which printer(s) were returned in your search?

_____

_____

5. Close the Find Printers windows.

▶ **To locate shared folders in Active Directory by using Active Directory Users And Computers**

1. In the console tree, right-click the *Domain*.contoso.msft node (where *Domain* is your assigned domain name), and then click Find.

2. In the Find Users, Contacts, And Groups dialog box, in the Find drop-down list, select Shared Folders.

3. In the Find Shared Folders dialog box, in the Keywords text box, type *computer* (where *computer* is your assigned computer name), and then click the Find Now button.

   Which shared folder(s) were returned in your search?

   _____

   _____

4. Click the Clear All button.

5. In the Find In The Directory message box, click OK.

6. In the Find Shared Folders dialog box, in the Keywords text box, type **Manufacturing**, and then click the Find Now button.

   Which shared folder(s) were returned in your search?

   _____

   _____

7. Close all open windows.

Exercise 3
Delegating Administration of Active Directory

In this exercise, you will delegate the administration of Active Directory.

▶ **To test permissions before delegating administration**

1. Log off as Administrator.

2. Log on to *domain* (where *domain* is your assigned domain name) as **johns** with a password of **password**.

3. Click Start, point to Programs, point to Administrative Tools, and then click Active Directory Users And Computers.

4. In the View menu, verify that the Advanced Features menu item is checked.

5. In the console tree, expand the *Domain*.contoso.msft node, expand the Contoso node, expand the IT node, and then select the IT node.

   In the Details pane, note the users and groups in the IT organizational unit.

6. In the Details pane, right-click Jim Carlyle, and then click Properties.

7. In the Jim Carlyle Properties dialog box, on the General tab, in the Description text box, type **IT Department Administrator**.

   Are you able to change the description information for Jim Carlyle?

   _____

8. In the Jim Carlyle Properties dialog box, open the Security tab.

   Are you able to change the security for Jim Carlyle?

   _____

9. Click the Cancel button.

10. In the console tree, expand the Manufacturing node, and then select the Manufacturing node.

    In the Details pane, note the users and groups in the Manufacturing organizational unit.

11. In the Details pane, right-click Linda Durell, and then click Properties.

12. In the Linda Durell Properties dialog box, on the General tab, in the Description text box, type **Manufacturing Department**.

    Were you able to change the description information for Linda Durell?

    _____

13. In the Linda Durell Properties dialog box, open the Security tab.

    Are you able to change the security for Linda Durell?

    _____

14. Click the Cancel button.

15. Close all open windows.

▶ **To delegate administration to the IT Department**

1. Log off as John Saunders.

2. Log on to *domain* (where *domain* is your assigned domain name) as **Administrator** with a password of **password**.

3. Click Start, point to Programs, point to Administrative Tools, and then click Active Directory Users And Computers.

4. In the console tree, expand the *Domain*.contoso.msft node, expand the IT node, and then select the IT node.

   In the Details pane, note the users and groups in the IT organizational unit.

5. In the console tree, right-click IT, and then click Delegate Control.

   The Delegation Of Control Wizard starts.

6. Use the information provided in the following table to complete the Delegation Of Control Wizard. You should accept defaults when no information is specified.

Wizard Page	Do the Following
Users Or Groups	Click the Add button. In the Select Users, Computers, Or Groups dialog box, select IT Department, click the Add button, and then click OK.
Tasks To Delegate	In the Delegate The Following Common Tasks list, select all the check boxes.

7. When the wizard completes, click the Finish button.

8. Close all open windows.

▶ **To test permissions after delegating administration**

1. Log off as Administrator.

2. Log on to *domain* (where *domain* is your assigned domain name) as **johns** with a password of **password**.

3. Using the previous procedures in this exercise, complete the tasks for each of the users listed in the following table. Record the success or failure of each task in the table.

Tip As a shortcut for finding the users, use Find in Active Directory Users And Computers to locate the users in Active Directory. Remember to start the search at *Domain*.contoso.msft (where *Domain* is your assigned domain name).

Task	Linda Durell	Meng Li	Jon Morris
View general information about the user on the General tab.			
On the General tab, in the Office text box, type *computer* (where *computer* is your assigned computer name).			
View security information on the Security tab.			
On the Security tab, remove the Write Personal Information permission from SELF.			

Were you able to perform all tasks for all users? If not, why were you unable to complete the tasks?

_____

_____

Exercise 4
Backing Up and Restoring Active Directory

In this exercise, you will back up and restore Active Directory.

▶ **To back up the domain controller's system state**

1. Log on to *domain* (where *domain* is your assigned domain name) as **Administrator** with a password of **password**.

2. Click Start, point to Programs, point to Accessories, point to System Tools, and then click Backup.

3. In the Backup–[Untitled] window, click Tools, and then click Options.

4. In the Options dialog box, on the Backup Log tab, select the Detailed option button, and then click OK.

5. In the Backup–[Untitled] window, click the Backup Wizard button.

   The Backup Wizard starts.

6. Use the information provided in the following table to complete the Backup Wizard. You should accept the defaults when no information is specified.

Wizard Page	Do the Following
What To Back Up	Select the Only Back Up The System State Data option button.
Where To Store The Backup	In the Backup Media Or File Name text box, type **d:\ADBackup.bkf**.

7. When the wizard completes, click the Finish button.

   The backup operation begins.

8. When the backup operation completes, in the Backup Progress dialog box, click the Report button.

   Review the backup log to see the files that are a part of the system state for a domain controller.

9. Close the log file.

10. In the Backup Progress dialog box, click the Close button.

11. Close the Backup–[Untitled] window.

▶ **To simulate the corruption of Active Directory**

1. Click Start, point to Programs, point to Administrative Tools, and then click Active Directory Users And Computers.

2. In the console tree, expand the *Domain*.contoso.msft node (where *Domain* is your assigned domain name), and then select the Training Course node.

   Note the users that exist in the Training Course organizational unit.

3. In the console tree, right-click the Training Course node, and then click Delete.

4. In the Active Directory message boxes, click the Yes button.

5. Close all open windows.

▶ **To restore the domain controller's system state**

1. Click Start, and then click Shutdown.

2. In the What Do You Want The Computer To Do? drop-down list, select Restart, and then click OK.

3. The computer shuts down and then restarts.

4. When the Boot Loader menu appears or when the message "For troubleshooting and advanced startup options for Windows 2000, press F8" appears, press F8.

5. In the Windows 2000 Advanced Option Menu screen, select Directory Services Restore Mode, and then press ENTER.

6. Log on as **Administrator** with a password of **password**.

7. In the Desktop message box, click OK.

8. Click Start, point to Programs, point to Accessories, point to System Tools, and then click Backup.

9. In the Backup–[Untitled] window, on the Welcome tab, click the Restore Wizard button.

The Restore Wizard starts.

10. Use the information provided in the following table to complete the Restore Wizard. You should accept the defaults when no information is specified.

Wizard Page	Do the Following
What To Restore	Expand the File node, expand the Media Created node, and then select the System State check box.

11. When the wizard completes, click the Finish button.

12. In the Enter Backup File Name dialog box, verify that D:\ADBackup.bkf appears in the Restore From Backup File text box, and then click OK.

The restore operation begins.

13. When the restore operation completes, in the Restore Progress dialog box, click the Close button.

A message box appears asking whether you want to restart your computer now.

14. In the Backup message box, click the No button.

15. Close all open windows.

▶   **To authoritatively restore Active Directory**

1. Click Start, and then click Run

2. In the Open box, type **cmd**, and then click OK.

3. At the command prompt, type **ntdsutil**, and then press ENTER.

4. At the ntdsutil: prompt, type **authoritative restore**, and then press ENTER.

5. At the authoritative restore: prompt, type **?**, and then press ENTER.

   Review the available options, especially Restore subtree.

6. At the authoritative restore: prompt, type **restore subtree "ou=Training Course, dc=*domain*, dc=contoso, dc=msft"** (where *domain* is your assigned domain name), and then press ENTER.

7. In the Authoritative Restore Confirmation Dialog message box, click the Yes button.

8. At the authoritative restore: prompt, type **quit**, and then press ENTER.

9. At the ntdsutil: prompt, type **quit**, and then press ENTER.

10. At the command prompt, type **exit**, and then press ENTER.

11. Click Start, and then click Shutdown.

12. In the What Do You Want The Computer To Do? drop-down list, select Restart, and then click OK.

13. The computer shuts down and then restarts.

▶   **To verify the restore of Active Directory**

1. Log on to *domain* (where *domain* is your assigned domain name) as **Administrator** with a password of **password**.

2. Click Start, point to Programs, point to Administrative Tools, and then click Active Directory Users And Computers.

3. In the console tree, expand the *Domain*.contoso.msft node.

   Note that the Training Course organizational unit is restored.

4. In the console tree, select the Training Course node.

   Note that the users that exist in the Training Course organizational unit are restored.

5. Close all open windows.

Lab 12: Administering Group Policy

Objectives

After completing this lab, you will be able to

- Implement group policies to manage desktop configurations.
- Delegate administration of Group Policy.
- Manage software by using Group Policy.
- Manage special folders by using Group Policy.

Before You Begin

To complete this lab, you need the following:

- The user accounts created in Lab 7.
- The group accounts created in Lab 8.

Users and Groups Used in This Lab

The following table lists the users and groups that are used in this lab's exercises. Refer to the table when you need to determine the user name, password, or group membership.

User	User Name	Password	Group Membership
John Saunders	johns	password	IT Department
Linda Durell	lindad	password	Manufacturing Department
Meng Li	mengli	password	Research Department
Louis Penna	louisp	password	Sales Department

Tip Remember that the IT Department group is a member of the Manufacturing Department, Sales Department, and Research Department groups.

Estimated time to complete this lab: 45 minutes

Exercise 1
Implementing Group Policies
to Manage Desktop Configuration

In this exercise, you will implement group policies to manage desktop configuration.

▶ **To assign group policies to domain controllers**

1. Log on to *domain* (where *domain* is your assigned domain name) as **Administrator** with a password of **password**.

2. Click Start, point to Programs, point to Administrative Tools, and then click Active Directory Users And Computers.

3. In the console tree, expand the *Domain*.contoso.msft node, and then select the Domain Controllers node.

4. In the console tree, right-click the Domain Controllers node, and then click Properties.

5. In the Domain Controllers Properties dialog box, on the Group Policy tab, click the New button.

   A New Group Policy Object entry appears in the list of group policies.

6. Change the name New Group Policy Object to **Advanced Domain Controllers Policy**.

7. Select Advanced Domain Controllers Policy, and then click the Edit button.

8. In the Group Policy console tree, expand the Computer Configuration node, expand the Windows Settings node, expand the Security Settings node, expand the Local Policies node, and then select the User Rights Assignment node.

9. In the Details pane, double-click Shut Down The System.

10. In the Security Policy Setting dialog box, select the Define These Policy Settings check box, and then click the Add button.

11. In the Add User Or Group dialog box, in the User And Group Names text box, type **Everyone**, and then click OK.

12. In the Security Policy Setting dialog box, click OK.

13. In the console tree, expand the Administrative Templates node, expand the System node, and then click Logon.

14. In the Details pane, double-click Delete Cached Copies Of Roaming Profiles.

15. In the Delete Cached Copies Of Roaming Profiles Properties dialog box, on the Policy tab, select the Enabled option button, and then click OK.

16. Close the Group Policy console.

17. In the Domain Controllers Properties dialog box, click the Close button.

▶ **To assign group policies to the Contoso organizational unit**

1. In the console tree, expand the *Domain*.contoso.msft node (where *Domain* is your assigned domain name), expand the Contoso node, and then select the Contoso node.

2. In the console tree, right-click the Contoso node, and then click Properties.

3. In the Contoso Properties dialog box, on the Group Policy tab, click the New button.

   A New Group Policy Object entry appears in the list of group policies.

4. Change the name New Group Policy Object to **Contoso OU Group Policy**.

5. Select Contoso OU Group Policy, and then click the Edit button.

6. In the Group Policy console tree, expand the User Configuration node, expand the Administrative Templates node, and then select the Start Menu & Taskbar node.

7. In the Details pane, double-click Add Logoff To The Start Menu.

8. In the Add Logoff To The Start Menu Properties dialog box, on the Policy tab, select the Enabled option button, and then click OK.

9. Close the Group Policy console.

10. In the Contoso Properties dialog box, click the Close button.

▶ **To implement a group policy for the IT organizational unit**

1. In the Active Directory Users And Computers console tree, expand the *Domain*.contoso.msft node (where *Domain* is your assigned domain name), expand the Contoso node, expand the IT node, and then select the IT node.

2. In the console tree, right-click IT, and then click Properties.

3. In the IT Properties dialog box, on the Group Policy tab, click the New button.

   A New Group Policy Object entry appears in the list of group policies.

4. Change the name New Group Policy Object to **IT OU Group Policy**.

5. Select IT OU Group Policy, and then click the Edit button.

6. In the Group Policy console tree, expand the User Configuration node, expand the Administrative Templates node, and then select the Start Menu & Taskbar node.

7. In the Details pane, double-click Add "Run In Separate Memory Space" Check Box To Run Dialog Box.

8. In the Add "Run In Separate Memory Space" Check Box To Run Dialog Box Properties dialog box, on the Policy tab, select the Enabled option button, and then click OK.

9. Close the Group Policy console.

10. In the IT Properties dialog box, click the Close button.

▶ **To implement a group policy for the Manufacturing organizational unit**

1. In the Active Directory Users And Computers console tree, expand the *Domain*.contoso.msft node (where *Domain* is your assigned domain name), expand the Contoso node, expand the IT node, expand the Manufacturing node, and then select the Manufacturing node.

2. In the console tree, right-click the Manufacturing node, and then click Properties.

3. In the Manufacturing Properties dialog box, on the Group Policy tab, click the New button.

   A New Group Policy Object entry appears in the list of group policies.

4. Change the name New Group Policy Object to **Manufacturing OU Group Policy**.

5. Select Manufacturing OU Group Policy, and then click the Edit button.

6. In the Group Policy console tree, expand the User Configuration node, expand the Administrative Templates node, and then select the Start Menu & Taskbar node.

7. In the Details pane, double-click Disable Logoff On The Start Menu.

8. In the Disable Logoff On The Start Menu Properties box, on the Policy tab, select the Enabled option button, and then click OK.

9. Close the Group Policy console.

10. In the Manufacturing Properties dialog box, click the Close button.

▶ **To implement group policy for the Sales organizational unit**

1. In the Active Directory Users And Computers console tree, expand the *Domain*.contoso.msft node (where *Domain* is your assigned domain name), expand the Contoso node, expand the IT node, expand the Sales node, and then select the Sales node.

2. In the console tree, right-click the Sales node, and then click Properties.

3. In the Sales Properties dialog box, on the Group Policy tab, click the New button.

   A New Group Policy Object entry appears in the list of group policies.

4. Change the name New Group Policy Object to **Sales OU Group Policy**.

5. Select Sales OU Group Policy, and then click the Edit button.

6. In the Group Policy dialog box, in the console tree, expand the User Configuration node, expand the Administrative Templates node, and then select the Desktop node.

7. In the Details pane, double-click Hide All Icons On Desktop.

8. In the Hide All Icons On Desktop Properties dialog box, on the Policy tab, select the Enabled option button, and then click OK.

9. Close the Group Policy console.

10. In the Sales Properties dialog box, click the Close button.

▶ **To test group policy for users**

1. Verify that the appropriate desktop settings are applied to each of the users listed in the following table by logging off and logging on as each user. Record the presence or absence of each desktop setting in the table.

Desktop Settings	John Saunders	Linda Durell	Meng Li	Louis Penna
Logoff is on the Start menu.				
Run In Separate Memory Space check box is in the Run dialog box.				
Icons are on desktop.				

Note The Run In Separate Memory Space check box is enabled only when you run 16-bit applications.

Did all users have all the desktop features? If not, why were some of the desktop features not available to certain users?

_____

_____

_____

_____

_____

2. Close all open windows.

Exercise 2
Delegating the Administration of Group Policies

In this exercise, you delegate the administration of group policies.

▶ **To delegate the administration of the IT OU group policy**

1. Log on to *domain* (where *domain* is your assigned domain name) as **Administrator** with a password of **password**.

2. Click Start, point to Programs, point to Administrative Tools, and then click Active Directory Users And Computers.

3. In the console tree, expand the *Domain*.contoso.msft node, expand the Contoso node, expand the IT node, and then select the IT node.

4. In the console tree, right-click the IT node, and then click Properties.

5. In the IT Properties dialog box, on the Group Policy tab, select IT OU Group Policy, and then click the Properties button.

6. In the IT OU Group Policy Properties dialog box, open the Security tab.

   Note the users and groups that already have permissions on IT OU group policy.

7. Click the Add button.

8. In the Select Users, Computers, Or Groups dialog box, select IT Department, click the Add button, and then click OK.

9. In the IT OU Group Policy Properties dialog box, on the Security tab, in the Permissions list, select the Allow check box in the Full Control row, and then click OK.

10. In the IT Properties dialog box, click Close.

▶ **To delegate the administration of the Sales OU group policy**

1. In the Active Directory Users And Computers console tree, expand the *Domain*.contoso.msft node (where *Domain* is your assigned domain name), expand the Contoso node, expand the IT node, expand the Sales node, and then select the Sales node.

2. In the console tree, right-click the Sales node, and then click Properties.

3. In the Sales Properties dialog box, on the Group Policy tab, select Sales OU Group Policy, and then click the Properties button.

4. In the Sales OU Group Policy Properties dialog box, open the Security tab.

   Note the users and groups that already have permissions on Sales OU group policy.

5. Click the Add button.

6. In the Select Users, Computers, Or Groups dialog box, select IT Department, click the Add button, and then click OK.

7. In the Sales OU Group Policy Properties dialog box, on the Security tab, in the Permissions list, select the Allow check box in the Full Control row, and then click OK.

8. In the Sales Properties dialog box, click OK.

9. Close all open windows.

▶ **To verify the delegation of administration to the IT Department group**

1. Log off as Administrator.

2. Log on to *domain* (where *domain* is your assigned domain name) as **johns** with a password of **password**.

3. Click Start, point to Programs, point to Administrative Tools, and then click Active Directory Users And Computers.

4. In the console tree, expand the *Domain*.contoso.msft node, expand the Contoso node, expand the IT node, and then select the IT node.

5. In the console tree, right-click the IT node, and then click Properties.

6. In the IT Properties dialog box, on the Group Policy tab, select IT OU Group Policy.

   What tasks can a member of the IT Department group complete (hint: look at the active buttons)?

   _____

   _____

7. Click the Properties button.

8. In the IT OU Group Policy Properties dialog box, on the General tab, select the Disable Computer Configuration Settings check box.

9. In the Confirm Disable message box, click the Yes button.

10. In the IT OU Group Policy Properties dialog box, click OK.

    Were you able to change the policy settings? Explain why you were or were not able to change the settings.

    _____

    _____

    _____

11. In the IT Properties dialog box, click OK.

12. Complete steps 4–8 for the Manufacturing OU group policy in the Manufacturing organizational unit.

    Were you able to change the policy settings for the Manufacturing OU? Explain why you were or were not able to change the settings.

_____

_____

_____

13. Complete steps 4–8 for the Sales OU group policy in the Sales OU.

    Were you able to change the policy settings for the Sales OU? Explain why you were or were not able to change the settings.

    _____

    _____

    _____

14. Close all open windows.

Exercise 3
Managing Software by Using Group Policy

In this exercise, you will manage software by using Group Policy.

▶ **To verify the software configuration prior to the software installation**

1. Log on to *domain* (where *domain* is your assigned domain name) as **johns** with a password of **password**.

2. Click Start, and then point to Programs.

   Verify that the Show Environment Variables menu folder does not appear on the Programs submenu.

▶ **To create a software distribution point**

1. Log off as johns.

2. Log on to *domain* (where *domain* is your assigned domain name) as **Administrator** with a password of **password**.

3. Click Start, and then click Run.

4. In the Open box, type **c:**, and then click OK.

5. In the Local Disk (C:) window, on the File menu, point to New, and then click Folder.

6. Name the new folder **SDPFolder**.

7. Right-click the SDPFolder folder, and then click Sharing.

8. In the SDPFolder Properties dialog box, select the Share This Folder option button; in the Share Name text box, type **SDPShare**, and then click the Permissions button.

9. In the Permissions For SDPShare dialog box, in the Permissions list, clear all check boxes except for the Allow check box in the Read row.

   The Everyone group should now have only Read permission on the SDPShare folder.

10. In the Permissions For SDPShare dialog box, click the Add button.

11. In the Select Users, Computers, Or Groups dialog box, select Administrators, click the Add button, and then click OK.

12. In the Permissions For SDPShare dialog box, select Administrators. In the Permissions list, select the Allow check box in the Full Control row, and then click OK.

13. In the SDPFolder Properties dialog box, click OK.

14. Close all open windows.

▶   **To copy software to the distribution point**

1. Click Start, and then click Run.

2. In the Open box, type **c:\setup**, and then click OK.

3. Click Start, and then click Run.

4. In the Open box, type **\\\computer\sdpshare** (where *computer* is your assigned computer name), and then click OK.

5. In the Setup window, right-click the MSIPackage folder, and then click Copy.

6. Right-click in the SDPShare On *Computer* window, and then click Paste.

   The MSIPackage folder is copied into the SDPShare folder.

7. Close all open windows.

▶   **To create a software distribution point**

1. Click Start, point to Programs, point to Administrative Tools, and then click Active Directory Users And Computers.

2. In the console tree, expand the *Domain*.contoso.msft node (where *Domain* is your assigned domain name), expand the Contoso node, right-click the Contoso node, and then click Properties.

3. In the Contoso Properties dialog box, on the Group Policy tab, click the New button.

   A New Group Policy Object entry appears in the list of group policies.

4. Change the name New Group Policy Object to **Software Distribution Group Policy**.

5. Select Software Distribution Group Policy, and then click the Edit button.

6. In the Group Policy console tree, expand the User Configuration node, expand the Software Settings node, and then select the Software Installation node.

7. Right-click the Software Installation node, and then click Properties.

8. In the Software Installation Properties dialog box, on the General tab, in the Default Package Location text box, type **\\\computer\SDPShare** (where *computer* is your assigned computer name).

9. Select the Uninstall The Applications When They Fall Out Of The Scope Of Management check box, and then click OK.

10. In the console tree, right-click the Software Installation node, point to New, and then click Package.

11. In the Open dialog box, in the File Name box, type **\\\computer\SDPShare\ MSIPackage\ShowEnv.msi**, and then click the Open button.

12. In the Deploy Software dialog box, select the Assigned option button, and then click OK.

13. In the console tree, select the Software Installation node.

    In the Details pane, notice the addition of the ShowEnv package.

    Close the Group Policy console.

14. In the Contoso Properties dialog box, click OK.

▶ **To install the assigned software**

1. Log off as Administrator.

2. Log on to *domain* (where *domain* is your assigned domain name) as **johns** with a password of **password**.

3. Click Start, point to Programs, point to Show Environment Variables, and then click ShowEnv.

    The Windows Installer automatically installs and starts the ShowEnv program.

4. In the Windows 2000 Environment Variables dialog box, click OK.

    The ShowEnv program displays the next list of environment variables.

5. In the Windows 2000 Environment dialog box, click OK.

Exercise 4
Managing Special Folders by Using Group Policy

In this exercise, you will manage special folders by using Group Policy.

▶ **To create a shared folder to host the special folders**

1. Log on to *domain* (where *domain* is your assigned domain name) as **Administrator** with a password of **password**.

2. Click Start, and then click Run.

3. In the Open box, type **c:**, and then click OK.

4. In the Local Disk (C:) window, on the File menu, point to New, and then click Folder.

5. Name the new folder **Special**.

6. Right-click the Special folder, and then click Sharing.

7. In the Local Disk (C:) Properties dialog box, select the Share This Folder option button, and then click OK.

8. Close all open windows.

▶ **To redirect special folders to a shared folder**

1. Click Start, point to Programs, point to Administrative Tools, and then click Active Directory Users And Computers.

2. In the console tree, expand the *Domain*.contoso.msft node (where *Domain* is your assigned domain name), expand the Contoso node, right-click the Contoso node, and then click Properties.

3. In the Contoso Properties dialog box, on the Group Policy tab, click the New button.

   A New Group Policy Object entry appears in the list of group policies.

4. Change the name New Group Policy Object to **Special Folder Group Policy**.

5. Select Special Folder Group Policy, and then click the Edit button.

6. In the Group Policy console tree, expand the User Configuration node, expand the Windows Settings node, and then expand the Folder Redirection node.

7. Right-click the Application Data node, and then click Properties.

8. In the Application Data Properties dialog box, on the Target tab, in the Setting drop-down list, select Basic–Redirect Everyone's Folder To The Same Location.

9. In the Target Folder Location text box, type ***computer*\Special\%user-name%\Application Data** (where *computer* is your assigned computer name), and then click OK.

10. Complete steps 7–9 for the Desktop folder.

11. Complete steps 7–9 for the My Documents folder.

12. Complete steps 7–9 for the Start Menu folder.

13. Close the Group Policy console.

14. In the Contoso Properties dialog box, click the Close button.

15. Close the Active Directory Users And Computers console.

▶   **To verify that special folders are redirected**

1. Log off as Administrator.

2. Log on to *domain* (where *domain* is your assigned domain name) as **johns** with a password of **password**.

3. On the desktop, double-click the My Documents icon.

4. In the My Documents window, on the File menu, point to New, and then click Text Document.

5. Name the new text document **MyFile**.

6. Close the My Documents window.

7. Click Start, and then click Run.

8. In the Open box, type *computer***special****johns** (where *computer* is your assigned computer name)**,** and then click OK.

   Did all the folders appear in the shared folder? If not, why are certain special folders absent from the shared folder?

   _____

   _____

   _____

9. In the Johns window, double-click My Documents.

   What documents appear in the My Documents window?

   _____

   _____

   _____

10. Close all open windows.

11. Log off as johns.

Lab 13: Administering a Security Configuration

Objectives

After completing this lab, you will be able to

- Audit access to files, folders, printers, and Active Directory objects.
- View and manage security logs.
- Grant rights to users and groups by using Group Policy.
- Analyze the security configuration of a domain controller by using the Security Configuration And Analysis console.

Before You Begin

To complete this lab, you need the following:

- Successful completion of Labs 7–12.

Users and Groups Used in This Lab

The following table lists the users and groups that are used in this lab's exercises. Refer to the table when you need to determine the user name, password, or group membership.

User	User Name	Password	Group Membership
John Saunders	johns	password	IT Department
Linda Durell	lindad	password	Manufacturing Department

Tip Remember that the IT Department group is a member of the Manufacturing Department, Sales Department, and Research Department groups.

Estimated time to complete this lab: 90 minutes

Exercise 1
Auditing Access to Files, Folders, Printers, and Active Directory Objects

In this exercise, you will configure auditing of access to files, folders, printers, and Active Directory objects.

▶ **To configure group policies for auditing**

1. Log on to *domain* (where *domain* is your assigned domain name) as **Administrator** with a password of **password**.

2. Click Start, point to Programs, point to Administrative Tools, and then click Active Directory Users And Computers.

3. In the console tree, expand the *Domain*.contoso.msft node, and then select the Domain Controllers node.

4. In the console tree, right-click the Domain Controllers node, and then click Properties.

5. In the Domain Controllers Properties dialog box, on the Group Policy tab, click the New button.

   A New Group Policy Object entry appears in the list of group policies.

6. Change the name New Group Policy Object to **Domain Controllers Audit Policy**.

7. Select Domain Controllers Audit Policy, and then continue to click the Up button until Domain Controllers Audit Policy is first in the list.

8. Select Domain Controllers Audit Policy, and then click the Edit button.

9. In the Group Policy dialog box, in the console tree, expand the Computer Configuration node, expand the Windows Settings node, expand the Security Settings node, expand the Local Policies node, and then select the Audit Policy node.

10. In the Details pane, double-click Audit Directory Service Access.

11. In the Security Policy Setting dialog box, select the Define These Policy Settings check box, select the Success check box, select the Failure check box, and then click OK.

12. In the Details pane, double-click Audit Logon Events.

13. In the Security Policy Settings dialog box, select the Define These Policy Settings check box, select the Failure check box, and then click OK.

14. In the Details pane, double-click Audit Object Access.

15. In the Security Policy Settings dialog box, select the Define These Policy Settings check box, select the Success check box, select the Failure check box, and then click OK.

16. Close the Group Policy console.

17. In the Domain Controllers Properties dialog box, click the Close button.

18. Close the Active Directory Users And Computers console.

▶ **To apply the audit policy to the domain controller**

1. Click Start, and then click Run.

2. In the Open box, type **cmd**, and then click OK.

3. At the command prompt, type **secedit /refreshpolicy machine_policy /enforce**, and then press ENTER.

4. At the command prompt, type **exit**, and then press ENTER.

5. Click Start, and then click Shutdown.

6. In the Shut Down Windows dialog box, in the What Do You Want The Computer To Do? drop-down list, select Restart, and then click OK.

   Your computer restarts.

▶ **To configure auditing for files and folders**

1. Log on to *domain* (where *domain* is your assigned domain name) as **Administrator** with a password of **password**.

2. Click Start, and then click Run.

3. In the Open box, type **c:\shares\manufact\prodschd**, and then click OK.

4. In the ProdSchd window, right-click the 1st-Qtr file, and then click Properties.

5. In the 1st-Qtr Properties dialog box, on the Security tab, click the Advanced button.

6. In the Access Control Settings For 1st-Qtr dialog box, on the Auditing tab, Click the Add button.

7. In the Select User, Computer, Or Group dialog box, select Everyone, and then click OK.

8. In the Auditing Entry For 1st-Qtr dialog box, use the settings in the following table to configure the auditing for the 1st-Qtr file. When no entry appears in the Successful or Failed column, you should leave the respective check box cleared.

Access	Successful	Failed
List Folder/Read Data		Checked
Read Attributes		Checked
Create Files/Write Data	Checked	Checked
Create Folders/Append Data		Checked
Write Attributes	Checked	Checked
Delete	Checked	Checked
Read Permissions		Checked
Change Permissions	Checked	Checked
Take Ownership	Checked	Checked

9. Click OK.

   Notice that the auditing entries are divided into two separate entries. What is the difference between these two entries?

   _____

   _____

10. In the Access Control Settings For 1st-Qtr dialog box, click OK.

    If you receive a warning message that says that the Audit Policy for the computer does not have auditing turned on, you should

    ■ Click OK.

    ■ At the end of this exercise, verify that you have properly completed the steps in the first procedure in this exercise.

    ■ At the end of this exercise, restart your computer before proceeding to the next exercise.

11. In the 1st-Qtr Properties dialog box, click OK.

12. Complete steps 3–10 for the 3rd-Qtr file in the ProdSchd folder.

13. Close the ProdSchd window.

▶ **To configure auditing for printers**

1. Click Start, point to Settings, and then click Printers.

2. In the Printers windows, right-click the HP LaserJet 4 icon, and then click Properties.

3 In the HP LaserJet 4 Properties dialog box, on the Security tab, click the Advanced button.

4. In the Access Control Settings For HP LaserJet 4 dialog box, on the Auditing tab, click the Add button.

5. In the Select User, Computer, Or Group dialog box, select Everyone, and then click OK.

6. In the Auditing Entry For HP LaserJet 4 dialog box, use the settings in the following table to configure the auditing for the HP LaserJet 4 printer. When

no entry appears in the Successful or Failed column, you should leave the respective check box cleared.

Access	Successful	Failed
Print	Checked	Checked
Manage Printers	Checked	Checked
Read Permissions	Checked	Checked
Change Permissions	Checked	Checked
Take Ownership	Checked	Checked

7. Click OK.

8. In the Access Control Settings For HP LaserJet 4 dialog box, click OK.

9. In the HP LaserJet 4 Properties dialog box, click OK.

10. Close the Printers window.

▶ **To configure auditing for Active Directory objects**

1. Click Start, point to Programs, point to Administrative Tools, and then click Active Directory Users And Computers.

2. In the Active Directory Users And Computers console, on the View menu, verify that the Advanced Features menu option is checked.

3. In the console tree, expand the *Domain*.contoso.msft node (where *Domain* is your assigned domain name), expand the Contoso node, and then select the Contoso node.

4. In the console tree, right-click the Contoso node, and then click Properties.

5. In the Contoso Properties dialog box, on the Security tab, click the Advanced button.

6. In the Access Control Settings For Contoso dialog box, on the Auditing tab, clear the Allow Inheritable Auditing Entries From Parent To Propagate To This Object check box.

   A Security message box appears.

7. In the Security message box, click the Copy button.

8. In the Access Control Settings For Contoso dialog box, on the Auditing tab, in the Auditing Entries list, select the first entry, and then click the View/Edit button.

9. In the Auditing Entry For Contoso dialog box, review the access that is being audited, and then click OK.

10. In the Access Control Settings For Contoso dialog box, click OK.

11. In the Contoso Properties dialog box, click OK.

12. Close the Active Directory Users And Computers console.

Exercise 2
Viewing and Managing Security Logs

In this exercise, you will view and manage security logs.

▶ **To clear the security logs**

1. Click Start, point to Programs, point to Administrative Tools, and then click Event Viewer.

2. In the Event Viewer console tree, select the Security Log node, right-click the Security Log node, and then click Clear All Events.

3. In the Event Viewer message box, click the No button.

4. Press F5.

5. In the Details pane, double-click Success Audit.

   The Event Properties dialog box appears. What caused the entry to be created in the Security Log?

   _____

   _____

6. In the Event Properties dialog box, click OK.

7. Close the Event Viewer console.

▶ **To create auditing entries for Active Directory events**

1. Log off as Administrator.

2. Attempt to log on to *domain* (where *domain* is your assigned domain name) as **InvalidUser** with a password of **password**.

   The logon attempt should fail.

3. Log on to *domain* as **johns** with a password of **password**.

4. Click Start, point to Programs, point to Administrative Tools, and then click Active Directory Users And Computers.

5. In the console tree, expand the *Domain*.contoso.msft node, expand the Contoso node, expand the IT node, and then select the Sales node.

6. In the Details pane, right-click Cindy Conners, and then click Properties.

7. In the Cindy Conners Properties dialog box, on the General tab, in the Office text box, type *computer* **Location** (where *computer* is your assigned computer name), and then click OK.

8. Close the Active Directory Users And Computers console.

▶ **To create auditing entries for file and folder events**

1. Click Start, and then click Run.

2. In the Open box, type **c:\shares\manufact\prodschd**, and then click OK.

3. In the ProdSchd window, right-click the 1st-Qtr file, and then click Properties.

4. In the 1st-Qtr Properties dialog box, on the Security tab, select Everyone. Select the Allow check box in the Read & Execute row, and then click OK.

5. Complete steps 3–4 for the 3rd-Qtr file.

6. Close the ProdSchd window.

▶ **To create auditing entries for printer events**

1. Click Start, point to Settings, and then click Printers.

2. In the Printers window, right-click the HP LaserJet 4 icon, and then click Properties.

3. In the HP LaserJet 4 Properties dialog box, open the Advanced tab, review the settings, and then click OK.

4. Close the Printers window.

▶ **To view the contents of the Security Log**

1. Log off as johns.

2. Log on to *domain* (where *domain* is your assigned domain name) as **Administrator**, with a password of **password**.

3. Click Start, point to Programs, point to Administrative Tools, and then click Event Viewer.

4. In the Event Viewer console tree, select the Security Log node.

   What can you determine about the tasks that have been attempted since you previously checked the Security Log?

   _____

   _____

   _____

   _____

   _____

▶ **To change the maximum size of the Security Log**

1. In the Event Viewer console tree, right-click the Security Log node, and then click Properties.

2. In the Security Log Properties dialog box, on the General tab, in the Maximum Log Size box, type **2048**, and then click the Apply button.

   What will happen when the Security Log reaches the value in the Maximum Log Size box?

   _____

   _____

▶   **To filter the contents of the Security Log**

1. In the Security Log Properties dialog box, on the Filter tab, in the Event Source drop-down list, select Security.

2. In the Category drop-down list, select Logon/Logoff, and then click OK.

3. Examine the entries in the Details pane.

   What entries appear in the Details pane?

   _____

   _____

4. In the Event Viewer console tree, right-click the Security Log node, and then click Properties.

5. In the Security Log Properties dialog box, on the Filter tab, in the Category drop-down list, select Directory Service Access, and then click OK.

6. Examine the entries in the Details pane.

   What entries appear in the Details pane?

   _____

   _____

7. In the Event Viewer console tree, right-click the Security Log node, and then click Properties.

8. In the Security Log Properties dialog box, on the Filter tab, in the Category drop-down list, select Object Access, and then click OK.

9. Examine the entries in the Details pane.

   What entries appear in the Details pane?

   _____

   _____

   _____

10. In the Event Viewer console tree, right-click the Security Log node, and then click Properties.

11. In the Security Log Properties dialog box, on the Filter tab, in the Event Source drop-down list, select All, and then click OK.

    Did the filters that you applied to the Security Log change the contents of the Security Log? Why or why not?

    _____

    _____

▶ **To clear and archive the Security Log**

1. In the Event Viewer console tree, right-click the Security Log node, and then click Clear All Events.

2. In the Event Viewer message box, click the Yes button.

3. In the Save "Security Log" As dialog box, click the Desktop button; in the File Name drop-down list, type **SecurityLog**; and then click the Save button.

4. In the Event Viewer console, on the Action menu, click Open Log File.

5. In the Open dialog box, click the Desktop button, and then select SecurityLog.evt.

6. In the Log Type drop-down list, select Security, and then click the Open button.

   In the Event Viewer console tree, the Saved Security Log node appears.

7. In the console tree, select the Saved Security Log node.

   In the Details pane, the events that you saved should appear.

8. Close the Event Viewer console.

9. Log off as Administrator.

Exercise 3
Assigning User Rights by Using Group Policy

In this exercise, you will assign rights to users and groups by using Group Policy.

▶ **To test user rights**

1. Log on to *domain* (where *domain* is your assigned domain name) as **lindad** with a password of **password**. Are you able to log on successfully? Why or why not?

   _____

   _____

2. Log off as lindad.

▶ **To grant rights to users by using Group Policy**

1. Log on to *domain* (where *domain* is your assigned domain name) as **Administrator** with a password of **password**.

2. Click Start, point to Programs, point to Administrative Tools, and then click Active Directory Users And Computers.

3. In the Active Directory Users And Computers console, on the View menu, verify that the Advanced Features menu option is checked.

4. In the console tree, expand the *Domain*.contoso.msft node, expand the Contoso node, and then select the Contoso node.

5. In the console tree, right-click the Contoso node, and then click Properties.

6. In the Contoso Properties dialog box, on the Group Policy tab, click the New button.

   A New Group Policy Object entry appears in the list of group policies.

7. Change the name New Group Policy Object to **User Rights Group Policy**.

8. Select User Rights Group Policy, and then continue to click the Up button until User Rights Group Policy is the first policy in the list.

9. Select User Rights Group Policy, and then click the Edit button.

10. In the Group Policy console tree, expand the Computer Configuration node, expand the Windows Settings node, expand the Security Settings node, expand the Local Policies node, and then select the User Rights Assignment node.

11. In the Details pane, double-click Deny Logon Locally.

12. In the Security Policy Setting dialog box, select the Define These Policy Settings check box, and then click the Add button.

13. In the Add User Or Group dialog box, click the Browse button.

14. In the Select Users Or Groups dialog box, select Linda Durell, click the Add button, and then click OK.

15. In the Add User Or Group dialog box, click OK.

16. In the Security Policy Setting dialog box, click OK.

17. Close the Group Policy console.

18. In the Contoso Properties dialog box, click the Close button.

19. Close the Active Directory Users And Computers console.

20. Click Start, and then click Shutdown.

21. In the Shut Down Windows dialog box, in the What Do You Want The Computer To Do? drop-down list, select Restart, and then click OK.

▶ **To verify the new user rights policies**

1. Log on to *domain* (where *domain* is your assigned domain name) as **lindad** with a password of **password**. Are you able to log on successfully? Why or why not?

   _____

   _____

2. Click Start, and then click Shutdown.

3. In the Shut Down Windows dialog box, in the What Do You Want The Computer To Do? drop-down list, select Restart, and then click OK.

Exercise 4
Analyzing the Security Configuration of a Domain Controller by Using the Security Configuration And Analysis Console

In this exercise, you will analyze the security configuration of a domain controller by using the Security Configuration And Analysis console.

▶ **To create a Security Templates console**

1. Log on to *domain* (where *domain* is your assigned domain name) as **Administrator** with a password of **password**.
2. Click Start, and then click Run.
3. In the Open box, type **mmc**, and then click OK.
4. On the Console menu, click Add/Remove Snap-in.
5. In the Add/Remove Snap-in dialog box, click the Add button.
6. In the Add Standalone Snap-in dialog box, select Security Templates, click the Add button, and then click the Close button.
7. In the Add/Remove Snap-in dialog box, click OK.
8. On the Console menu, click Options.
9. In the Options dialog box, in the Console Mode drop-down list, select User Mode—Limited Access, Single Window, and then click OK.
10. On the Console menu, click Save As.
11. In the Save As dialog box, in the Save In drop-down list, select Desktop.
12. In the File Name text box, type **Security Templates**, and then click the Save button.
13. Close all open windows.

▶ **To create a Security Configuration and Analysis console**

1. Click Start, and then click Run.
2. In the Open box, type **mmc**, and then click OK.
3. On the Console menu, click Add/Remove Snap-in.
4. In the Add/Remove Snap-in dialog box, click the Add button.
5. In the Add Standalone Snap-in dialog box, select Security Configuration And Analysis, click the Add button, and then click the Close button.
6. In the Add/Remove Snap-in dialog box, click OK.
7. On the Console menu, click Options.

8. In the Options dialog box, in the Console Mode drop-down list, select User Mode—Limited Access, Single Window, and then click OK.

9. On the Console menu, click Save As.

10. In the Save As dialog box, in the Save In drop-down list, select Desktop.

11. In the File Name text box, type **Security Configuration and Analysis**, and then click the Save button.

12. Close all open windows.

▶ **To define a new security template**

1. On the desktop, double-click the Security Templates icon.

2. In the Security Templates console tree, expand the Security Templates node, right-click the c:\WINNT\Security\Templates node, and then click New Template.

3. In the c:\WINNT\Security\Templates dialog box, in the Template Name text box, type **Contoso Security Template**.

4. In the Description text box, type **Security template used for all computers within Contoso, Ltd.**, and then click OK.

5. In the console tree, expand the c:\WINNT\Security\Templates node, expand the Contoso Security Template node, expand the Account Policies node, and then select the Password Policy node.

6. In the Details pane, double-click Minimum Password Length.

7. In the Template Security Policy Setting dialog box, select the Define This Policy Setting In The Template check box.

8. In the Password Must Be At Least box, type **8**, and then click OK.

9. In the Details pane, double-click Minimum Password Age.

10. In the Template Security Policy Setting dialog box, select the Define This Policy Setting In The Template check box.

11. In the Password Can Be Changed After box, type **10**, and then click OK.

12. In the Suggested Value Changes dialog box, click OK.

13. Close the Security Templates console.

14. In the Save Security Templates dialog box, click the Yes button.

▶ **To analyze the security configuration of a domain controller**

1. On the desktop, double-click the Security Configuration And Analysis icon.

2. In the Security Configuration And Analysis console, in the console tree, right-click the Security Configuration And Analysis node, and then click Open Database.

3. In the Open Database dialog box, in the File Name text box, type **Contoso Security Database**, and then click the Open button.

4. In the Import Template dialog box, select Contoso Security Template, and then click the Open button.

5. In the console tree, right-click the Security Configuration And Analysis node, and then click Configure Computer Now.

6. In the Configure System dialog box, note the path and file name of the error log, and then click OK.

7. In the console tree, right-click the Security Configuration And Analysis node, and then click Analyze Computer Now.

8. In the Perform Analysis dialog box, note the path and file name of the error log, and then click OK.

9. In the console tree, expand the Security Configuration And Analysis node, expand the Account Policies node, and then select the Password Policy node.

    Do the current settings of the domain controller match the settings in the security template?

    _____

    _____

10. In the Details pane, double-click Minimum Password Age.

11. In the Analyzed Security Policy Setting dialog box, in the Password Can Be Changed After box, type **15**, and then click OK.

    Do the current settings of the domain controller match the settings in the security template?

    _____

    _____

12. Close the Security Configuration And Analysis console.

13. In the Save Security Templates dialog box, click the Yes button.

14. Close all open windows.

Lab 14: Managing Active Directory Performance

Objectives

After completing this lab, you will be able to

- Remove an existing Active Directory forest.
- Create child domains in an existing Active Directory forest.
- Verify trust relationships between domains.
- Monitor domain controller performance by using the Performance console.
- Monitor replication by using Replication Monitor and the repadmin utility.

Before You Begin

The following table lists the computer names, domains, fully qualified domain names (FQDNs), and IP addresses that have been decided for Contoso, Ltd. Your instructor will provide you with the value for *x*, which is your assigned classroom number.

Computer Name	Domain	FQDN	IP Address
Chicago	usa-a	chicago.usa-a.contoso.msft	192.168.x.101
Atlanta	usa-a	atlanta.usa-a.contoso.msft	192.168.x.102
Boston	usa-b	boston.usa-b.contoso.msft	192.168.x.103
San Jose	usa-b	sanjose.usa-b.contoso.msft	192.168.x.104
Montreal	canada-a	montreal.canada-a.contoso.msft	192.168.x.105
Toronto	canada-a	toronto.canada-a.contoso.msft	192.168.x.106
Vancouver	canada-b	vancouver.canada-b.contoso.msft	192.168.x.107
Edmonton	canada-b	edmonton.canada-b.contoso.msft	192.168.x.108
Paris	west-europe-a	paris.west-europe-a.contoso.msft	192.168.x.109
Brussels	west-europe-a	brussels.west-europe-a.contoso.msft	192.168.x.110
Madrid	west-europe-b	madrid.west-europe-b.contoso.msft	192.168.x.111
London	west-europe-b	london.west-europe-b.contoso.msft	192.168.x.112
Bonn	east-europe-a	bonn.east-europe-a.contoso.msft	192.168.x.113
Rome	east-europe-a	rome.east-europe-a.contoso.msft	192.168.x.114
Stockholm	east-europe-b	stockholm.east-europe-b.contoso.msft	192.168.x.115
Vienna	east-europe-b	vienna.east-europe-b.contoso.msft	192.168.x.116
Moscow	asia-a	moscow.asia-a.contoso.msft	192.168.x.117
New Delhi	asia-a	newdelhi.asia-a.contoso.msft	192.168.x.118
Hong Kong	asia-b	hongkong.asia-b.contoso.msft	192.168.x.119
Tokyo	asia-b	tokyo.asia-b.contoso.msft	192.168.x.120
Sydney	south-pacific-a	sydney.south-pacific-a.contoso.msft	192.168.x.121
Melbourne	south-pacific-a	melbourne.south-pacific-a.contoso.msft	192.168.x.122
Auckland	south-pacific-b	auckland.south-pacific-b.contoso.msft	192.168.x.123
Manila	south-pacific-b	manila.south-pacific-b.contoso.msft	192.168.x.124

Estimated time to complete this lab: 120 minutes

Exercise 1
Removing an Existing Active Directory Forest

In this exercise, you will remove your existing Active Directory forest.

▶ **To remove Active Directory from your computer**

1. Log on to *domain* (where *domain* is your assigned domain name) as **Administrator** with a password of **password**.

2. Click Start, and then click Run.

3. In the Open box, type **dcpromo.exe**, and then click OK.

   The Active Directory Installation Wizard starts.

4. Use the information provided in the following table to complete the Active Directory Installation Wizard. You should accept the defaults when no information is specified.

Wizard Page	Do the Following
Remove Active Directory	Select the This Server Is The Last Domain Controller In The Domain check box.
Network Credentials	In the User Name text box, type **Administrator**.
	In the Password text box, type **password**.
Administrator Password	In the Password and Confirm Password text boxes, type **password**.

5. When the wizard completes, click the Finish button.

   A dialog box appears, prompting you to restart the computer so that the changes you made can take effect.

6. Click the Restart Now button.

   The computer restarts.

▶ **To remove DNS from your computer**

1. Log on to your computer as **Administrator** with a password of **password**.

2. Click Start, point to Settings, and then click Control Panel.

3. In the Control Panel window, double-click the Add/Remove Programs icon.

4. In the Add/Remove Programs dialog box, click the Add/Remove Windows Components button.

   The Windows Components Wizard starts.

5. On the Windows Components page, in the Components list, select Networking Services, and then click the Details button.

6. In the Subcomponents Of Networking Services list, clear the Domain Name System (DNS) check box, and then click OK.

7. In the Windows Components Wizard, click Next.

8. Click the Finish button to complete the Windows Components Wizard.

9. Close the Add/Remove Programs dialog box.

10. Close the Control Panel window.

▶   **To configure TCP/IP to use the instructor's DNS server**

1. On the desktop, right-click the My Network Places icon, and then click Properties.

2. In the Network And Dial-up Connections window, right-click the Local Area Connection icon, and then click Properties.

3. In the Local Area Connection Properties dialog box, select Internet Protocol (TCP/IP), and then click the Properties button.

4. In the Preferred DNS Server address box, type **192.168.*x*.100** (where *x* is your assigned classroom number), and then click OK.

5. In the Local Area Connection Properties dialog box, click OK.

6. Close the Network And Dial-Up Connections window.

▶   **To configure the DNS suffix for your computer**

1. On the desktop, right-click the My Computer icon, and then click Properties.

2. In the System Properties dialog box, on the Network Identification tab, click the Properties button.

3. In the Identification Changes dialog box, click the More button.

4. In the DNS Suffix And NetBIOS Computer Name dialog box, in the Primary DNS Suffix Of This Computer text box, type ***domain*.contoso.msft** (where *domain* is your assigned domain name for this lab), and then click OK.

5. In the Identification Changes dialog box, click OK.

6. In the Network Identification message box, click OK.

7. In the System Properties dialog box, click OK.

8. In the System Settings Change message box, click the Yes button.

   The system restarts.

▶   **To verify the proper TCP/IP configuration**

1. Log on to your computer as **Administrator** with a password of **password**.

2. Click Start, and then click Run.

3. In the Open box, type **cmd**, and then click OK.

4. At the command prompt, type **ipconfig /all**, and then press ENTER.

5. Verify that the value of Host Name is your assigned host name.

6. Verify that the value of Primary DNS Suffix is the full domain name assigned to your computer.

7. Verify that the value of DNS Servers is 192.168.*x*.100 (where *x* is your assigned classroom number).

8. At the command prompt, type **exit**, and then press ENTER.

Exercise 2
Create Child Domains in an Existing
Active Directory Forest

In this exercise, you and your partner will create a child domain in the existing contoso Active Directory forest.

▶   **To install the first domain controller in the child domain**

Important Perform this procedure only on the computer with the lower IP address between you and your partner. For example, if your IP address ends in .109 and your partner's IP address ends in .110, you will complete this procedure.

---

1. Click Start, and then click Run.

2. In the Open box, type **dcpromo.exe**, and then click OK.

   The Active Directory Installation Wizard starts.

3. Use the information provided in the following table to complete the Active Directory Installation Wizard. You should accept the defaults when no information is specified.

Wizard Page	Do the Following
Domain Controller Type	Select the Domain Controller For New Domain option button.
Create Tree Or Child Domain	Select the Create A New Child Domain In An Existing Domain Tree option button.
Network Credentials	In the User Name text box, type **Administrator**.
	In the Password text box, type **password**.
	In the Domain text box, type **contoso.msft**.
Child Domain Installation	Click the Browse button.
	In the Browse For Domain dialog box, select contoso.msft, and then click OK.
	In the Child Domain text box, type *domain* (where *domain* is your assigned domain name).
NetBIOS Domain Name	Verify that *DOMAIN* appears.
Permissions	Select the Permissions Compatible Only With Windows 2000 Servers option button.
Directory Services Restore Mode Administrator Password	In the Password and Confirm Password text boxes, type **password**.

4. When the wizard completes, click the Finish button.

   A dialog box appears, prompting you to restart the computer so that the changes you made can take effect.

5. Click the Restart Now button.

   The computer restarts.

6. Log on to *domain* as **Administrator** with a password of **password**.

▶ **To install the second domain controller in the child domain**

Important Perform this procedure only on the computer with the higher IP address between you and your partner. For example, if your IP address ends in .109 and your partner's IP address ends in .110, your partner will complete this procedure.

---

1. Click Start, and then click Run.

2. In the Open box, type **dcpromo.exe**, and then click OK.

   The Active Directory Installation Wizard starts.

3. Use the information provided in the following table to complete the Active Directory Installation Wizard. You should accept the defaults when no information is specified.

Wizard Page	Do the Following
Domain Controller Type	Select the Additional Domain Controller For An Existing Domain option button.
Network Credentials	In the User Name text box, type **Administrator**.
	In the Password text box, type **password**.
	In the Domain text box, type *domain* (where *domain* is your assigned domain name).
Additional Domain Controller	Click the Browse button.
	In the Browse For Domain dialog box, select *Domain*.Contoso.msft, and then click OK.
Directory Services Restore Mode Administrator Password	In the Password and Confirm Password text boxes, type **password**.

4. When the wizard completes, click the Finish button.

   A dialog box appears, prompting you to restart the computer so that the changes you made can take effect.

5. Click the Restart Now button.

   The computer restarts.

6. Log on to *domain* as **Administrator** with a password of **password**.

7. In the Windows 2000 Configure Your Server window, clear the Show This Screen At Startup check box, and then close the Windows 2000 Configure Your Server window.

Exercise 3
Verifying Trust Relationships Between Domains

In this exercise, you will verify the trust relationships between domains in the contoso forest.

▶ **To verify the trust relationship between your child domain and contoso.msft**

1. Click Start, point to Programs, point to Administrative Tools, and then click Active Directory Domains And Trusts.

2. In the console tree, expand the Contoso.msft node, select the *Domain*.contoso.msft node (where *Domain* is your assigned domain name), right-click the *Domain*.Contoso.msft node, and then click Properties.

3. In the *Domain*.contoso.msft Properties dialog box, open the Trusts tab.

   What trust relationships exist between your child domain and other domains?

   _____

   _____

   _____

4. In the Domains Trusted By This Domain list, select Contoso.msft, and then click the Edit button.

5. In the Contoso.msft Properties dialog box, click the Verify button.

6. In the Active Directory dialog box, in the User Name text box, type **Administrator**.

7. In the Password text box, type **password**, and then click OK.

Tip You may receive a message indicating that the trust relationship failed between your domain controller and the instructor's domain controller. If you receive this message, perform the SC reset to retry establishing the trust relationship.

---

8. A message appears indicating the trust has been verified. Click OK.

9. In the Contoso.msft Properties dialog box, click OK.

10. In the *Domain*.contoso.msft Properties dialog box, click OK.

11. Close the Active Directory Domains And Trusts console.

▶ **To install the Windows 2000 Support Tools**

1. Click Start, and then click Run.

2. In the Open box, type **\\newyork\support\tools\setup**, and then click OK.

   The Welcome To The Windows 2000 Support Tools Setup Wizard starts.

3. Complete the Windows 2000 Support Tools Setup Wizard by accepting the default values for all wizard pages.

4. When the wizard completes, click the Finish button.

▶ **To verify the trust relationship by using the netdom tool**

1. Click Start, and then click Run.

2. In the Open box, type **cmd**, and then click OK.

3. At the command prompt, type **netdom help trust**, and then press ENTER.

   Review the syntax of the netdom command.

4. At the command prompt, type **netdom trust** *domain* **/domain:contoso /userd:administrator /passwordd:password /usero:administrator /passwordo:password /verify** (where *domain* is your assigned domain name), and then press ENTER.

   The netdom utility returns the current status of the trust relationship.

5. At the command prompt, type **exit**, and then press ENTER.

6. Close any open windows.

Exercise 4
Monitoring Domain Controller Performance
by Using the Performance Console

In this exercise, you will monitor domain controller performance by using the Performance console.

▶ **To configure the Performance console to monitor Active Directory**

1. Click Start, point to Programs, point to Administrative Tools, and then click Performance.

2. In the console tree, select the System Monitor node.

3. Right-click in the Details pane, and then click Add Counters.

4. In the Add Counters dialog box, in the Performance Object drop-down list, select NTDS.

5. In the Select Counters From List box, select DRA Inbound Bytes Total/sec, and then click the Add button.

6. Add the counters in the following list to the Performance console:

   ■ NTDS : DRA Inbound Object Updates Remaining in Packet

   ■ NTDS : DRA Outbound Bytes Total/sec

   ■ NTDS : DRA Pending Replication Synchronizations

   ■ NTDS : LDAP Bind Time

   ■ NTDS : LDAP Client Sessions

   ■ NTDS : LDAP Searches/sec

7. In the Add Counters dialog box, click the Close button.

8. Minimize the Performance console.

▶ **To generate Active Directory activity**

1. Click Start, point to Programs, point to Administrative Tools, and then click Active Directory Users And Computers.

2. In the Active Directory Users And Computers console, expand the *Domain*.contoso.msft node (where *Domain* is your assigned domain name), and then select the Domain Controllers node.

3. In the Details pane, right-click *Computer* (where *Computer* is your assigned computer name), and then click Properties.

4. Maximize the Performance console.

   Which counters have been affected by running the Active Directory Users And Computers console?

   _____

   _____

5. Minimize the Performance console.

6. In the *Computer* Properties dialog box, click the Cancel button.

▶ **To prepare for bulk import of user accounts**

1. In the Active Directory Users And Computers console tree, expand the *Domain*.contoso.msft node (where *Domain* is your assigned domain name), select the *Domain*.contoso.msft node, right-click the *Domain*.Contoso.msft node, point to New, and then click Organizational Unit.

2. In the New Object–Organizational Unit dialog box, in the Name text box, type **computer** (where *computer* is your assigned computer name), and then click OK.

3. Minimize the Active Directory Users And Computers console.

4. Click Start, and then click Run.

5. In the Open box, type **c:\setup\dsusers.txt**, and then click OK.

6. In the DSUsers–Notepad window, replace all occurrences of domain with your assigned domain name.

7. Replace all occurrences of computer with your assigned computer name.

8. Replace all occurrences of ## with the last octet (byte) of your assigned IP address. For example, if your IP address is 192.168.*x*.103, you would replace ## with 103.

9. Save the edited file, and then close the DSUsers–Notepad window.

▶ **To generate Active Directory activity by using bulk import of users**

1. Click Start, and then click Run.

2. In the Open box, type **cmd**, and then click OK.

3. At the command prompt, type **c:**, and then press ENTER.

4. Type **cd setup**, and then press ENTER.

5. Type **csvde -i -f dsusers.txt**, and then press ENTER.

   The csvde utility reports that 22 entries were successfully modified.

6. Close the Command Prompt window.

7. Maximize the Performance console.

   Which counters have been affected by running the bulk import of users command?

   _____

   _____

   _____

   _____

   _____

8. Close the Performance console.

9. Close all open windows.

Exercise 5
Monitoring Domain Controller Replication

In this exercise, you will monitor the replication between domain controllers in your domain by using Replication Monitor and the repadmin utility.

▶ **To monitor replication by using Replication Monitor**

1. Click Start, point to Programs, point to Windows 2000 Support Tools, point to Tools, and then click Active Directory Replication Monitor.

2. In the console tree, right-click the Monitored Servers node, and then click Add Monitored Server.

3. In the Add Server To Monitor dialog box, select the Add The Server Explicitly By Name option button, and then click Next.

4. In the Enter The Name Of The Server To Monitor Explicitly text box, type *computer* (where *computer* is your assigned computer name), and then click the Finish button.

   Which directory partitions are replicated to your domain controller?

   _____

   _____

   _____

   _____

   _____

5. Expand each replication directory partition node and examine the replication partners for each partition.

6. Right-click *Computer* node, and then click Show Replication Topologies.

7. In the View Replication Topology window, on the View menu, click Connection Objects Only.

8. Right-click the *Computer* icon, and then click Show Intra-Site Connections.

   Lines are drawn to your domain controller that represent your inbound replication connections.

9. Close the View Replication Topology window.

10. In the Active Directory Replication Monitor console tree, right-click the *Computer* node, and then click Properties.

11. In the Server Properties dialog box, open the Server Flags tab.

    Note the properties that are enabled for the domain controller.

12. Open the FSMO Roles tab.

Note the list of operation master role holders as known by this domain controller.

13. Open the Inbound Replication Connections tab.

Examine the list of descriptions of why the connection objects were established.

14. Click OK.

15. Close the Active Directory Replication Monitor console.

▶ **To monitor replication by using the repadmin utility**

1. Click Start, and then click Run.

2. In the Open box, type **cmd**, and then click OK.

3. At the command prompt, type **repadmin /?**, and then press ENTER.
Examine the syntax of the repadmin utility.

4. At the command prompt, type **repadmin /showreps**, and then press ENTER.
When was the last schema directory replication made?

_____

_____

Why was the last schema directory replication made?

_____

_____

5. At the command prompt, type **exit**, and then press ENTER.

6. Close all open windows.

Lab 15: Deploying Microsoft Windows 2000 by Using Remote Installation Services (RIS)

Objectives

After completing this lab, you will be able to

- Install and configure RIS.
- Create a RISPrep image.
- Create a RIS boot disk.
- Verify the configuration of RIS.
- Deploy Microsoft Windows 2000 Professional to desktop computers by using RIS (optional).
- Find RIS client computers in Active Directory after they have been deployed (optional).

Estimated time to complete this lab: 120 minutes

Exercise 1
Installing and Configuring RIS

In this exercise, you will install and configure RIS on your domain controller.

Important Perform this exercise only on the computer with the higher IP address between you and your partner. For example, if your IP address ends in .109 and your partner's IP address ends in .110, your partner will complete this procedure.

▶ **To add the RIS component to your computer**

1. Log on to *domain* (where *domain* is your assigned domain name) as **Administrator** with a password of **password**.

2. Click Start, point to Settings, and then click Control Panel.

3. In the Control Panel window, double-click the Add/Remove Programs icon.

4. In the Add/Remove Programs window, click the Add/Remove Windows Components button.

   The Windows Components Wizard starts.

5. In the Windows Components Wizard, on the Windows Components page, in the Components list, select the Remote Installation Services check box, and then click Next.

6. If prompted for the Windows 2000 Server distribution files, type **\\newyork\i386**.

   The appropriate files are copied.

7. Click the Finish button to complete the Windows Components Wizard.

8. In the Add/Remove Programs window, click the Close button.

9. Close the Control Panel window.

   Wait for the System Settings Change message box to appear.

10. In the System Settings Change message box, click the Yes button.

    The computer restarts.

▶ **To authorize RIS in your domain**

1. Log on to contoso as **Administrator** with a password of **password**.

2. Click Start, point to Programs, point to Administrative Tools, and then click DHCP.

3. In the DHCP console tree, select the DHCP node.

4. On the Action menu, click Manage Authorized Servers.

5. In the Manage Authorized Servers dialog box, click the Authorize button.

6. In the Authorize DHCP Server dialog box, type **computer** (where *computer* is your assigned computer name), and then click OK.

   Your computer appears in the list of authorized DHCP servers.

7. In the Manage Authorized Servers dialog box, click the Close button.

8. Close the DHCP console.

▶ **To configure RIS on your computer**

1. Log on to *domain* (where *domain* is your assigned domain name) as **Administrator** with a password of **password**.

2. Click Start, point to Settings, and then click Control Panel.

3. In the Control Panel window, double-click the Add/Remove Programs icon.

4. In the Add/Remove Programs window, click the Add/Remove Windows Components button.

5. In the Add/Remove Programs dialog box, in the Set Up Services list, select Configure Remote Installation Services, and then click the Configure button.

   The Remote Installation Services Setup Wizard starts.

6. Use the information provided in the following table to complete the Remote Installation Services Setup Wizard. You should accept the defaults when no information is specified.

Wizard Page	Do the Following
Remote Installation Folder Location	Type **D:\RemoteInstall**.
Installation Source Files Location	Type **\\newyork\win2kpro**.

Note The process for copying the Windows 2000 Professional source files to your server will take about 20 minutes to complete.

7. When the wizard completes, click the Done button.

8. Close all open windows.

▶ **To configure the RIS server properties**

1. Click Start, point to Programs, point to Administrative Tools, and then click Active Directory Users And Computers.

2. In the console tree, expand the *Domain*.contoso.msft node (where *Domain* is your assigned domain name), expand the Domain Controllers node, and then select the Domain Controllers node.

3. In the Details pane, right-click *Computer* (where *Computer* is your assigned computer name), and then click Properties.

4. In the *Computer* Properties dialog box, on the Remote Install tab, select the Respond To Client Computers Requesting Service check box.

5. Click the Advanced Settings button.

6. In the *Computer*-Remote-Installation-Services Properties dialog box, on the New Clients tab, select the The Following Directory Service Location option button, and then click the Browse button.

7. In the Browse For A Directory Service Folder dialog box, expand the Contoso node, expand the *Domain* node, select the Computers node, and then click OK.

8. In the *Computer*-Remote-Installation-Services Properties dialog box, on the Images tab, note the installation image that you created during the installation of RIS, and then click OK.

9. In the *Computer* Properties dialog box, click OK.

► **To set the client installation options**

1. In the Active Directory Users And Computers console tree, expand the *Domain*.contoso.msft node (where *Domain* is your assigned domain name), and then select the Domain Controllers node.

2. Right-click the Domain Controllers node, and then click Properties.

3. In the Domain Controllers Properties dialog box, on the Group Policy tab, select Default Domain Controller Policy, and then click the Edit button.

4. In the Group Policy console tree, expand the User Configuration node, expand the Windows Settings node, and then select the Remote Installation Services node.

5. In the Details pane, double-click Choice Options.

6. In the Choice Options Properties dialog box, under Automatic Setup, select the Allow option button.

7. Under Custom Setup, select the Allow option button.

8. Under Restart Setup, select the Allow option button.

9. Under Tools, select the Allow option button, and then click OK.

10. Close the Group Policy console.

11. In the Domain Controllers Properties dialog box, click OK.

12. Close all open windows.

► **To set the client installation options**

1. On the desktop, right-click the My Computer icon, and then click Explore.

2. In the My Computer window, navigate to the D:\RemoteInstall\Setup \English\Images\Win2000.pro\I386\Templates folder.

3. In the file system tree, right-click the Templates node, and then click Properties.

4. In the Templates Properties dialog box, on the Security tab, verify that the Everyone group has Read & Execute, List Folder Contents, and Read permissions, and then click OK.

Exercise 2
Creating a RISPrep Image

In this exercise, you and your partner will create a RISPrep image that you can distribute to desktop computers.

Important Perform this exercise only on the computer with the lower IP address between you and your partner. For example, if your IP address ends in .109 and your partner's IP address ends in .110, you will complete this procedure.

▶ **To prepare the installation image**

1. Shut down your computer, and then restart with Windows 2000 Professional.
2. Log on as **Administrator** with a password of **password**.
3. Click Start, and then click Run.
4. In the Open text box, type *your_partner's_computer*\reminst\admin \i386\riprep.exe (where *your_partner's_computer* is your partner's assigned computer name), and then click OK.

   The Remote Installation Preparation Wizard starts.
5. Use the information provided in the following table to complete the Remote Installation Preparation Wizard. You should accept the defaults when no information is specified.

Wizard Page	Do the Following
Folder Name	In the Folder Name text box, type **RISImages**.
Friendly Description And Help Text	In the Friendly Description text box, type **Images used by RIS**.
	In the Help Text box, type **Images used by RIS for the deployment of Windows 2000 Professional**.

Note The process for creating the RISPrep image will take about 30–40 minutes to complete.

During the process of downloading the RISPrep image, the computer will restart.

Once the computer has restarted, an abbreviated version of the Windows 2000 Professional Setup Wizard starts.

6. Use the information provided in the following table to complete the Windows 2000 Professional Setup Wizard. You should accept the defaults when no information is specified.

Wizard Page	Do the Following
License Agreement	Select the I Accept This Agreement option button.
Personalize Your Software	In the Name text box, type *w2kpro_name* (where *w2kpro_name* is your assigned Windows 2000 Professional computer name).
	In the Organization text box, type **Contoso, Ltd**.
Computer Name And Administrator Password	In the Computer Name text box, type *w2kpro_name*.
	In the Administrator Password and Confirm Password text boxes, type **password**.
Date And Time Settings	Adjust the date, time, and time zone to match your date and time settings.
Networking Settings	Select the Custom Settings option button.
Workgroup Or Computer Domain	Select the Yes, Make This Computer A Member Of The Following Domain option button.
	In the Workgroup Or Computer Domain text box, type **CONTOSO**.
	In the Join Computer To CONTOSO Domain dialog box, in the User Name text box, type **Administrator**.
	In the Password text box, type **password**.

7. When the wizard completes, click the Finish button.

   The computer restarts.

8. Use the information provided in the following table to complete the Network Identification Wizard. You should accept the defaults when no information is specified.

Wizard Page	Do the Following
User Account	Select the Do Not Add A User At This Time option button.

9. When the wizard completes, click the Finish button.

10. Log on as **Administrator** with a password of **password**.

11. Click Start, and then click Shut Down.

12. In the Shut Down Windows dialog box, click OK.

The student computer shuts down.

Exercise 3
Creating a RIS Boot Disk

In this exercise, you and your partner will create a boot diskette that you can use to start the RIS process.

Important Perform this exercise only on the computer with the higher IP address between you and your partner. For example, if your IP address ends in .109 and your partner's IP address ends in .110, your partner will complete this procedure.

▶ **To create a RIS boot diskette**

1. Verify that you have a blank, formatted diskette.

2. Click Start, and then click Run.

3. In the Open text box, type ***computer*\reminst\admin\i386\rbfg.exe** (where *computer* is your assigned computer name), and then click OK.

4. Insert the blank formatted diskette into the disk drive.

5. In the Windows 2000 Remote Boot Disk Generator dialog box, select the Drive A option button, and then click the Create Disk button.

   The Windows 2000 Remote Boot Disk Generator verifies the diskette, removes any existing files, and then writes the RIS boot disk files to the diskette.

6. In the Windows 2000 Remote Boot Disk Generator information box, click the No button.

7. In the Windows 2000 Remote Boot Disk Generator dialog box, click the Close button.

8. Remove the RIS boot diskette from the disk drive.

Exercise 4
Verifying and Administering the Configuration of RIS

In this exercise, you and your partner will verify and administer the configuration of RIS on your domain controller.

Important Perform this exercise only on the computer with the higher IP address between you and your partner. For example, if your IP address ends in .109 and your partner's IP address ends in .110, your partner will complete this procedure.

▶ **To modify the product ID in the RIPREP.SIF file**

1. On the desktop, right-click the My Computer icon, and then click Explore.

2. In the My Computer window, browse to the D:\RemoteInstall\Setup \English\Images\RISImages\I386\Templates folder.

3. In the Details pane, double-click the RIPREP.SIF file.

4. In the Open With dialog box, select Notepad, and then click OK.

5. In the RIPREP.SIF–Notepad window, in the [UserData] section, type **ProductID = "VXKC4-2B3YF-W9MFK-QB3DB-9Y7MB"**.

6. On the File menu, click Save.

7. Close the RIPREP.SIF–Notepad window.

▶ **To verify the configuration of RIS on your domain controller**

1. Click Start, point to Programs, point to Administrative Tools, and then click Active Directory Users And Computers.

2. In the console tree, expand the *Domain*.contoso.msft node (where *Domain* is your assigned domain name), and then select the Domain Controllers node.

3. In the Details pane, right-click *Computer* (where *Computer* is your assigned computer name), and then click Properties.

4. In the *Computer* Properties dialog box, on the Remote Install tab, click the Verify Server button.

   The Remote Installation Services Setup Wizard starts.

5. Use the information provided in the following table to complete the Remote Installation Services Setup Wizard. You should accept the defaults when no information is specified.

Wizard Page	Do the Following
Remote Installation Services Verification Complete	Verify that no errors were found in the RIS server configuration.

6. When the wizard completes, click the Finish button.

7. In the Remote Installation Services Setup Wizard dialog box, click the Done button.

8. In the *Computer* Properties dialog box, click OK.

▶ **To prestage a client computer**

1. In the console tree, expand the *Domain*.contoso.msft node (where *Domain* is your assigned domain name), and then select the Computers node.

2. Right-click the Computers node, point to New, and then click Computer.

3. In the New Object–Computer dialog box, in the Computer Name and Computer Name (Pre-Windows 2000) text boxes, type *your_partner's_ w2kpro_name* (where *your_partner's_w2kpro_name* is your partner's assigned Windows 2000 Professional computer name), and then click Next.

4. In the Managed dialog box, select the This Is A Managed Computer check box, and in the Computer's Unique ID (GUID/UUID) text box, type *guid* (where *guid* is the GUID of your partner's computer).

Important If your partner's computer does not have a GUID, RIS will create a GUID by preceding the MAC address of the network adapter with 20 zeros. For example, if the MAC address of the network adapter is 00-50-DA-65-41-C1, RIS will create a GUID of {00000000-0000-0000-0000-0050DA6541C1}. If you are uncertain about whether the computers in your classroom have GUIDs, ask your instructor.

Tip You can type **ipconfig /all** from a command prompt to determine the MAC address of the network adapter in your computer.

---

5. In the Managed dialog box, click Next.

6. In the Host Server dialog box, select the The Following Remote Installation Server option button.

7. In the The Following Remote Installation Server text box, type *computer* (where *computer* is your assigned computer name), and then click Next.

8. In the New Object–Computer dialog box, review the settings, and then click the Finish button.

Exercise 5 (Optional)
Deploying Windows 2000 to
Desktop Computers by Using RIS

In this optional exercise, you and your partner will deploy the RISPrep image of Windows 2000 by using RIS.

Note If the network adapters in your classroom are not supported by the RIS boot disk, or the network adapters are not Pre-Boot eXecution Environment (PXE)–compatible, then you will not be able to complete this exercise.

Important Perform this exercise only on the computer with the lower IP address between you and your partner. For example, if your IP address ends in .109 and your partner's IP address ends in .110, you will complete this procedure.

▶ **To deploy Windows 2000 Professional to desktop computers**

1. Shut down your computer.

2. Place the RIS boot diskette in the disk drive, and then start your computer.

Note The RIS boot diskette will time out quickly, so be prepared to press F12 when the message is displayed.

The Windows 2000 Remote Installation Boot Floppy welcome message is displayed. The DHCP message appears followed by the TFTP message.

3. Press F12.

The Client Installation Wizard is started, and the Welcome To The Client Installation Wizard screen is displayed.

4. Use the information provided in the following table to complete the Client Installation Wizard. You should accept the defaults when no information is specified.

Wizard Page	Do the Following
Type a valid user name, password, and domain name.	In the User Name text box, type **Administrator**. In the Password text box, type **password**. In the Domain text box, type *domain* (where *domain* is your assigned domain name).
Use the arrow keys to select one of the following operating systems.	Select Images Used By RIS.
The following settings will be applied to this computer installation.	Remove the RIS boot diskette from the drive.

The wizard starts the Text Mode portion of the Windows 2000 setup.

Note The installation of Windows 2000 Professional can take 30–45 minutes to complete.

The computer finishes copying the files and then restarts. After the computer restarts, an abbreviated version of the Windows 2000 Professional Setup Wizard starts.

5. Use the information provided in the following table to complete the Windows 2000 Professional Wizard. You should accept defaults when no information is specified.

Wizard Page	Do the Following
Personalize Your Software	In the Name text box, type *w2kpro_name* (where *w2kpro_name* is your assigned Windows 2000 Professional computer name).

6. When the wizard completes, click the Finish button.

   The computer restarts.

7. Log on as **Administrator** with a password of **password**.

8. Click Start, and then click Shut Down.

9. In the Shut Down Windows dialog box, click OK.

   The computer shuts down.

Exercise 6 (Optional)
Finding RIS Client Computers

In this optional exercise, you and your partner will find RIS client computers after they have been deployed.

Note If the network adapters in your classroom are not supported by the RIS boot disk, or the network adapters are not Pre-Boot eXecution Environment (PXE)-compatible, then you will not be able to complete this exercise.

Important Perform this exercise only on the computer with the higher IP address between you and your partner. For example, if your IP address ends in .109 and your partner's IP address ends in .110, your partner will complete this procedure.

▶ **To find RIS client computers**

1. Click Start, point to Programs, point to Administrative Tools, and then click Active Directory Users And Computers.

2. In the console tree, expand the *Domain*.contoso.msft node (where *Domain* is your assigned domain name), right-click the *Domain*.contoso.msft node, and then click Find.

3. In the Find Users, Contacts, And Groups dialog box, in the Find box, click Remote Installation Clients.

4. In the Find Users, Contacts, And Groups dialog box, in the GUID text box, type *GUID* (where *GUID* is the first four digits of your partner's GUID), and then click Find Now.

Important If your partner's computer does not have a GUID, RIS will create a GUID by preceding the MAC address of the network adapter with 20 zeros. For example, if the MAC address of the network adapter is 00-50-DA-65-41-C1, RIS will create a GUID of {00000000-0000-0000-0000-0050DA6541C1}. If you are uncertain about whether the computers in your classroom have GUIDs, ask your instructor.

The newly deployed Windows 2000 Professional computer is returned.

5. In the list of computers found in the search, double-click *Your_partner's_w2kpro_name* (where *Your_partner's_w2kpro_name* is your partner's assigned Windows 2000 Professional computer name).

6. In the *Your_partner's_w2kpro_name* Properties dialog box, open the Remote Install tab.

   Which computer is the Remote Installation Server for the Windows 2000 Professional computer?

   _____

   _____

7. Click the Cancel button.

8. Close the Find Users, Contacts, And Groups dialog box.

9. Close the Active Directory Users And Computers console.